WOOLWORTHS

THE CHANGE IN TIMES OF WOOLWORTHS SOUTH AFRICA

by

Charles Nesbitt

Dedicated to the memory of

Doreen Lilian Nesbitt

(1918-1980)

Copyright ©2018 by Charles Nesbitt. All rights reserved.

ISBN: 9781728900261
Imprint: Independently published

Also by Charles Nesbitt

FUNDAMENTALS FOR SUCCESSFUL AND SUSTAINABLE FASHION BUYING AND MERCHANDISING
*
FUNDAMENTALS FOR FASHION RETAIL STRATEGY PLANNING AND IMPLEMENTATION
*
FUNDAMENTALS FOR FASHION RETAIL ARITHMETIC, MERCHANDISE ASSORTMENT PLANNING AND TRADING
*
FUNDAMENTALS OF FASHION RETAIL, TECHNOLOGY, MANUFACTURING AND SUPPLIER MANAGEMENT
*
THE COMPLETE JOURNAL OF FASHION RETAIL BUYING AND MERCHANDISING
*
RETAIL FASHION PROCUREMENT TEAM ROLES AND PROCESSES
*
RETAIL FASHION SCENARIO AND STRATEGY PLANNING
*
RETAIL FASHION ARITHMETIC
*
RETAIL FASHION MASTER DATA MANAGEMENT
*
RETAIL FASHION MERCHANDISE ASSORTMENT PLANNING AND TRADING
*
RETAIL FASHION MANUFACTURING AND TECHNOLOGY
*
RETAIL FASHION SUPPLIER MANAGEMENT
*
RETAIL FASHION PRODUCT STORAGE AND LOGISTICS

Table of Contents

PREFACE 4

IN THE BEGINNING 5

THE BOND TO MARKS AND SPENCER AND THE INFLUENCES THEREOF 8

LIFE IN THE SHADOW OF MARKS AND SPENCER 13

EARLY COMPUTERISATION 24

ORGANISATIONAL STRUCTURES 26

THE MERGER AND CREATION OF WOOLTRU 29

    THE MAYOR'S GARDEN 30

    THE IMPACT OF THE MERGER ON WOOLWORTHS 31

LEADERSHIP ERAS 32

RESOURCING OVERSEAS AND EXTERNAL LOCAL LEADERSHIP/MANAGEMENT 35

FRANCHISE STORES – THE DOWNFALL 40

SYSTEMS DEVELOPMENT 41

THE WOOLWORTHS CARD 45

THE CHANGE FROM MERCHANDISE LED TO BUYING LED BUSINESS 45

THE CHANGE OF SUPPLER BASE PHILOSOPHIES 48

QUALITY AND INNOVATION 53

LOGISTICAL APPROACHES AND EFFECTS OF GLOBAL SOURCING 55

    CROSS DOCK OR FLOW THROUGH MODEL 55

    WAREHOUSED PRODUCT 56

SHIFT TO PROCUREMENT OF NEW GLOBAL BUSINESSES 58

THE WAY FORWARD 60

REFERRALS AND ACKNOWLEDGEMENTS 62

PREFACE

Thirty five years of my life was spent at Woolworths South Africa where I was exposed to the majority of the key disciplines of the company which included an initial period of two years in a number of stores before being drafted into Head Office.

In Head Office I spent much of my time in clothing as part of the buying teams across virtually all the various textile buying groups as well as the foods division where eight years was spent followed by an extensive period in the clothing Central Merchandising division in various capacities which encompassed planning, heading up a support team and playing an integral part in some significant projects which were implemented across the business. Included in the role was the responsibility for the operational relationship with the main stream functions in both textiles and foods and the other service divisions such as Logistics, IT, Marketing, Technology after which I went on to create an operational group dedicated to the overall management of suppliers.

Given this, it is evident that I was able to enjoy a wide exposure across the breadth of the business which serves as the base that I have used to document my experiences and comments on significant events, strategy shifts and the organisational structure resources which impacted on the successes and failures.

This base has been intertwined with the history of the business spanning across a period of time which is from the inception of the company to the modern day existence.

Coupled to the above, in my birth year of 1952 my mother, Doreen Nesbitt, joined Woolworths at the same time that David Susman took over the reins and she spent the next 25 years as the buyer of children's clothing. It is therefore no surprise that most of our family dinner conversations were supplemented with discussions about Woolworths and thus was very much part of my life growing up.

Reference is made in the book to the autobiography of the founder, Max Sonnenberg's book "The way I saw it". Well if I can be bold enough, this book in the same essence could have also been titled "The way I saw It" except I was not the founder, nor was I a chairman, director or an executive but a pure and simple middle manager. While I did gain a wide exposure to the business I often proudly refer to myself as to having started my career at the bottom and finishing it at the bottom! This is the perspective from which the book is written.

The book describes the early beginnings of Woolworths, South Africa, how the association with Marks and Spencer UK evolved and the relationships that came with it. The philosophies and operational methodologies as well as some of the interesting characters who steered Woolworths through this period are also commented on.

The merger with Truworths was a momentous milestone in the history of Woolworths especially in the way that this event influenced the culture and brought a number of new structural changes and operational objectives.

Apart from relationship changes there were notable modifications as to the way business was conducted. Some of the most significant events that had major effects on the way business was conducted were as follows:

The change of a merchandising led to a buying managed approach business.

The introduction of the computerisation age to the Woolworths environment.

The launch of the Woolworths card and it's explosive effect on trade.

The development and implementation of sophisticated IT systems with the challenges that accompanied this happening.

The franchising of the brand and the complications that accompanied the initiative.

The change of the sourcing policies from a local dominant industry to an offshore supplier base which, although came with major benefits it also eventually brought many unforeseen costs and operational challenges.

An aggressive overseas corporates acquisition strategy saw a move to expand the stable of stores and new trademark names that probably had the most significant impact on the brand philosophies of the company.

In hindsight these initiatives and others which will be shared in the book were very brave challenges embarked on by many innovative individuals whose roles will be touched on and the successful or not so fruitful influences will be portrayed during the journey.

IN THE BEGINNING

Max Sonnenberg was born in the German city of Kaiserslautern on the third of May in 1879. His father Louis Sonnenberg was a school teacher but later tried to improve his wealth by engaging in ventures in both commerce and industry. Max Sonnenberg had two older and two younger sisters.

It was his well-known Uncle Ikey who was the inspiration for Max Sonnenberg' s family to eventually move to South Africa. In 1849 Uncle Ikey emigrated to America and where he engrossed himself for a long time in the tough mining camps in the far west in a quest for gold. This was followed by a stretch in the Northern Army during the Civil War.

He maintained very little communication with his family in Germany where nevertheless, his mother also encouraged his younger brother Charlie to follow Ikey.

Charlie was unsuccessful in tracking down Ikey, but coincidentally he also volunteered for the Northern Army during the civil war where, like his brother, he also accomplished a fine military career. It was on the battlefields of Gettysburg that the two coincidentally met after a lapse of seventeen years and subsequently completed the campaign together.

Ikey however, could not settle down after the war and in 1867 after hearing that diamonds had been discovered in the Cape of Good Hope he undertook the long voyage to South Africa where he joined the River Diggings on the Vaal river.

Charlie followed him to South Africa and together with a German kinsman he set up a business in Queenstown, but generally spent most of his time with Ikey pursuing a race to make his fortune in a new diamond rush which became to be known as Kimberley.

In the meanwhile, a third brother, Joseph, had come out from Germany to join them. Things had gone quite well and Charlie decided to sell out his mining interests to an upcoming young man who was none other than Cecil John Rhodes.

Around about 1893 when there was a considerable Sonnenberg family presence in South Africa.

Max's father decided to emigrate to South Africa and join the family business and after young Max donated his special stamp collection towards the costs, he and his father departed for South Africa. Soon after their arrival they journeyed to Kimberley where the activity at the Big Hole had diminished considerably so they moved onto Vryburg which was a small village with a population of about 3000 situated at the end of the main railway line to the north.

Solomon & Co was the dominant trading store in the town which belonged to Uncle Charlie trading in farming implements and lucratively serving the black market in the main with many patterned blankets and shawls which were especially produced for the firm by overseas manufacturers. The position of Vryburg at the railway terminus gave it a new importance when, with the opening up of Rhodesia, the railway to Bulawayo was constructed and together with the expansion of direct lines to Cape, Natal and Lourenco Marques enabled a new rail line to Johannesburg and subsequently with it, Vryburg and Solomon & Co flourished. It was therefore in Vryburg where Max Sonnenberg accepted the offer of his Uncle Charlie to start his working career and develop his deep interest in politics to the extent that eventually he stood for parliament. Unfortunately Max failed contesting the 1924 election and later went on to establish his business of Sonnenberg Ltd. in Mossel Bay. The business eventually became dormant in the town.

While visiting Cape Town in 1925 he heard that a business of Eaton Roberts & Co. were in liquidation and was up for sale. Max visited his long standing friend Sir de Villiers Graaf who agreed to back him in his wish to acquire the company. Thus Sonnenberg Ltd. became the buyer and he converted the premises in St. Georges street into a departmental store as Sonnenberg Ltd.

Max Sonnenberg very quickly found out that his store continued to trade with the original Eaton and Roberts values which was primarily catering for the wealthy clientele with good quality reasonably priced goods but the turnover remained to be substandard. Max put this down to a lack of an appropriate offer to the middle range of customers who lived and shopped mostly for cash in the surrounding areas of his store.

On a trip to England he sought out an old friend of his, Percy Lewis and who had become the managing director of the Buying Office for Woolworths Limited of Australia and New Zealand, a successful chain of stores unrelated to F. W. Woolworths. Percy Lewis was keen for Max to establish a chain in the same format as that in Australia and New Zealand and sell the similar range of goods which would ideally suit market that Max was targeting in South Africa. With little hesitation they established a new concern known as African Chain Stores Limited in London to procure the goods as was done for Woolworths Limited.

Back in South Africa, with some difficulty, Max registered the name Woolworths in Pretoria and from there the chain of Woolworths in South Africa known today to millions today affectionately as "Woolies" was born.

At the bottom of Plein Street in the heart of the most popular lower priced retail shopping area, the old Royal Hotel had recently closed down and hence the opportunity to utilise the disused dining room presented itself. It was in this location which had a frontage onto Plein street and stretched right through to Corporation street that the first Woolworths opened its doors on 31st of October in 1931

The first Woolworths store in the stately dining room of the Royal Hotel

(source: Wikipedia)

Three years later, a second branch opened in Durban, with another two, in Port Elizabeth and Johannesburg, opening a year later. Since then, Woolworths has consistently expanded and built its reputation for superior quality, exciting innovation and excellent value through constant expansion of its footprint across the width and breadth of South Africa.

Max's son Richard who had recently qualified as a chartered accountant was placed in charge of office administration assisted by Fred Kossuth. A young man who had worked for CTC Bazaars, Harry Saevetson, was appointed as the store manager and enjoyed a long illustrious career with the company. As a young student I worked in the holidays in the Plein Street store when Harry Saevetson was still the manager. At the same time, Nellie Price who was a Sales Assistant in the Royal Hotel dining room in 1931 and appears in the photograph (above) when Woolworths opened its doors was my Supervisor and when I was a Departmental Manager in the store in 1977, Nellie was still there and her function was to procure the cakes for the staff that may be celebrating their birthday.

Richard went on to become the Chairman of the company up until the late seventies.

African Chain Stores Limited continued to use Australasian Chain Stores as their buyers and shippers in London until 1950 at which point Woolworths opened their own buying office in London.

In 1947 a revolutionary event took place in Woolworths almost by accident. While Max and his family were travelling abroad, his wife and daughters befriended some girls who were related to one of the chain store magnates of Great Britain , namely Israel M Sieff, one of the figureheads behind the 230 store strong Marks & Spencer Ltd. which was a household name in every part of the United Kingdom.

Although the interaction was initially purely social, it eventually led to Max meeting the Chairman, Sir Simon Marks and shortly after their interaction they developed a close friendship.

It was through this relationship that a deal was agreed upon whereby a very close association between the South African Woolworths and Marks & Spencer was established. All the vast buying, financial and other facilities at the disposal of Marks & Spencer was made available to Woolworths. Initially there was a financial linkage in that M&S secured 90,000 ordinary shares and 96,000 "A" shares in Woolworths Holdings which represented the entire unissued share capital.

THE BOND TO MARKS AND SPENCER AND THE INFLUENCES THEREOF

In 1948 Sir Simon Marks set off to South Africa to visit the new business that he had invested in. He brought with him a high powered deputation which apart from his wife included the M&S Finance and Store Operations directors and their wives, Marcus Sieff (later Lord Sieff), two nephews of Sir Simon and a director of the largest supplier of M&S. The group included Ann Laskie, a niece of Sir Simon.

David Susman, the son of Elie Susman, was a young man of 22. He was educated at a Methodist school in Grahamstown and thereafter spent a year at Witwatersrand University until he was eighteen and was enlisted into the army where he went on to serve as trooper in the Natal Carbineers during the Italian campaign. He was demobilised in 1946 and returned to university to complete a degree in commerce. Having worked part time in the Woolworths Johannesburg office he had gained a deep insight into the business and developed some strong viewpoints of the company . At the time of the visit of the deputation he was a student on vacation and was active in the office. Regarding the visit of the group to Cape Town he noted the impact by saying that there can never have been a more effective and professional group under the dynamic leadership of Sir Simon himself.

The group worked sometimes twelve hours a day in stores and head office critically analysing figures, the goods as well as their composition, store layouts including the fixtures and the meagre control systems. Sir Simon rubbished the merchandise and the senior management of the time, terrifying the buyers and store management who were often reduced to states of gibbering incoherence.

It was only natural that the Johannesburg Office headed up by Elie Susman and his team where David Susman worked part time apprehensively anticipated the visit of what was described as the travelling circus.

However, the visit went off surprisingly well. Hymie Wolffe, who was in charge of administration recalled that they were mainly impressed with his accounting systems and in particular his primitive calculating machine which ensured that stock take results were available in a matter of days rather than months. It was insisted that he be transferred to head office where he soon became the company secretary and eventually a director. This is the position he held when I entered Head Office as a trainee merchandiser in the Lingerie departments and coincidentally reported to his son Michael Wolffe. Michael was besotted with his personal computer which was a relatively new innovation to the world at the time and he took great joy in demonstrating to me how it could measure your biorhythms. Truth be known he was considered a bit of an eccentric in this regard but after hearing the story of his father and his primitive calculating machine makes me appreciate the fact that often the apple does not fall too far from the tree.

David travelled with the group and was mesmerised with Sir Simons lamenting about retailing night after night as they dined and expressing his views on the potential of Woolworths if only if it were to absorb and apply the principles of M&S. One evening when he was having a drink in the suite of Sir

Simon at the Carlton Hotel and David was expressing his views of the shortcomings of Woolworths, Sir Simon asked him to write him a note in this regard.

Together with his good friend Jeff Perlman he spent the rest of the night writing "Woolworths (Pty) Limited: A brief outline as a basis to the future policy". Because there was a request to keep it short, the note was condensed to three pages wherein they focused on the topics such as false economies, shortage of trained staff and unwillingness to dispose of bad stock and emphasised the need for centralised allocation of counter space, feature lines and window displays and the use of professionally printed ticketing in order that store managers could focus on the provision of maximum superb service and attention to the customer. Sir Simon was highly impressed with the manuscript and it is assumed that it formed the basis for the fondness that Sir Simon developed for David and in turn David had no doubt that Sir Simon's powerful personality, his uncompromising standards and philosophies to business had the most profound influence in his own life.

Personally I can relate to this. I was a departmental manager in the newly opened major flagship store in Adderley Street in the mid-seventies when he was due to visit the store, for which I had prepared and prepared over again. When David Susman and his entourage were ushered into my area where I was nervously standing at attention, he walked straight to a counter and took an upside down ticket out of the frame and replaced it the right way up. I was shattered that I missed that detail (retail is detail) and was in hope that the floor would swallow me up. It was during this visit that he pointed to a square floor tile and proceeded to painfully explain to me while the entourage listened attentively to the principle as to how that tile represented money which should be respected in the way proportionate displays need to demand the amount of space they occupy dependent on their sales performance. That was a lesson that I never forgot throughout my career.

The visit of Sir Simon Marks had other impacts on David Susman's life. The contact with the overseas visitors made him increasingly aware of the developments in Palestine even though the Susman's already had close ties to Palestine and Zionism and were among the international backers of Chaim Weizmann and David Ben-Gurion who were to become the first president and first prime minister of Israel. When there was an anticipated war of independence after the end of the British mandate, Ben Gurion requested Marcus Sieff to set up a logistical supply plan. War did break out in May 1948 and David Susman was one the many South Africans to volunteer for service. Unfortunately he was wounded in conflict and returned to South Africa for medical treatment.

Sometime before he went back to Palestine at a function for the delegation held by Richard and Cecelia Sonnenberg he met Ann Laski and they found that they got on well together. Unfortunately Ann had to return to England with the visiting group. David and Anne kept in touch by letter and a year later they met again when David passed through England on his return to Israel after recovering from his injuries. After two days they became engaged and three weeks later they were married. They departed for Israel where they spent two years during which David was transferred from the military over to the diplomatic corps. During this time Simon, named after Sir Simon Marks was born in 1950.

The plan was that they would return to England where David would spend a period of two years before returning to South Africa and Woolworths. This they did in August 1950.

Upon his arrival in England David was put on an accelerated version of the M&S training courses for management trainees during which he spent time in stores, notably the second largest store in the chain, the Pantheon in Oxford street. He was also sent on attachment to some of the major suppliers to learn about fibres, yarns and manufacturing processes where he developed a fascination for the merchandise. The last period was spent in the Head Office in Baker street.

It was in this time that he became acutely aware of the deteriorating relationship between M&S and Woolworths. It had not gone to plan as envisioned in 1947. Max Sonnenberg's health slumped to the stage that he withdrew from day to day management in 1949 and the burden of control fell on his son Richard who severely felt the effects of the burden of the task.

Consequently the value of the shares dropped quite dramatically. The M&S envoys sent to instil the M&S philosophies had failed miserably and the constricted measures of the new Nationalist government tightened up controls of the importation of goods. As a result Woolworths was receiving a much smaller quota of M&S ranges. Sir Simon Marks was exasperated and was seriously considering the sale of his shares to Sam Cohen of OK Bazaars and others at the time.

It was at this point that David Susman vigorously defended the Sonnenbergs and Woolworths arguing that Sir Simon was sending the inappropriate people to South Africa to rectify the challenges and that they needed younger people with more energy and talent to inspire Woolworths into action.

The response, after some consideration, resulted in Sir Simon conceding that David was right.

In the light of this conversation David Susman drafted the future plans whereby in April 1952 he would return to Woolworths for two months. Two or three of Woolworths young men would return with him back to M&S for six months for intensive training after which they would return to South Africa augmented by one or two members of M&S head office. David was to stay with his team and remain on for five or six years before returning to London. The return however did not happen in that he never returned after the five or six years but stayed on for no less than fifty years as the general manager from 1952, as managing director from 1956, chairman from 1983 and president from 1993 to 2002.

There was one of the M&S members of the team that came out with David Susman who I suspect was a gentleman known as Mick Levy. When I entered head office in the seventies I was exposed to the legendry Mick Levy and was informed that he was David Susman's right hand man and was his eyes and ears. To put it mildly he was feared by all the merchandisers of the time. He carried no title, was situated in a modest small work place on the second floor of the old head office not far from David Susman's office, he dressed modestly and drove a dilapidated Mini Minor.

Mick Levy prowled the corridors of the old head office and if you were lucky enough to spot him first and was able to duck into a doorway you would be able to avoid his barking questions or instructions. It was not uncommon to return to your desk after lunch and find Mick slouched over your desk checking your figures in your production book. The production book was a Merchandiser's big black book, which, in the absence of computers was the only planning tool modelled on that used at M&S. For this reason, apart from the need to have extra long arms to carry it, special wider desks were issued to merchandisers so the book did not fall off the end.

The books had to be kept meticulously neat and were the main reference manuscript in merchandise reviews where they were interrogated and analysed to the utmost degree. David Susman was always accompanied by Mick Levy and sat at his side during such appraisals.

During one such review, which was extremely tense with important representatives from all over the business making it all quite intimidating, Mick commandeered my precious pride and joy production book. He proceeded to attack the pages with a stubby pencil with a point that had long last seen a sharpener and started scribbling over the pages with big circles and arrows with comments that left me devastated. Obviously my look of horror was quite evident, so much so that David Susman asked me what was wrong. Too shocked to be able to produce an answer, my boss at the time croaked out that Mick was writing all over the production book. David Susman, in his soft spoken manner which nevertheless was quite stern and clearly conveyed the message said "Mr Levy is the one person who is allowed to do anything he wants in this business".

On another occasion when my department was in serious trouble in that there were no size small panties in stores to such an extent that the situation had become quite a controversial issue throughout the company. Mick Levy burst into our office and stormed to my desk roaring "your size small panties". At this point I had no doubt that I would be packing up all my humble possessions into a brown box and would be exiting the business that day. Sitting in front of me he called the buyer at the time to bring him twelve size small panties and twelve size medium panties. As The Plein street store was below head office he instructed me to go down to the counter where they sold pick and mix sweets by weight and weigh each bundle of panties. The shoppers were very bemused at this embarrassed young man weighing ladies panties on the sweet scale. After recording my findings, I returned anxiously to my desk. I presented him with my conclusions which reflected a negligible variance. He looked at me and said to my great relief "You see ! They weigh the same so you don't have a size small problem!" True merchant thinking and life returned to normal with not much noise being heard about my size small problem again.

Our relationship took a weird turn when he started a habit of walking into our office every now and then without a word would drop his read overseas newspapers on my desk. This continued for many months and as I had only visited England once, I never knew quite why.

I was privileged in later years when he retired but still had a desk in the building which he shared with another counterpart legend Harry Stein, he would call on me to come and brief him and Harry as to what is going on in the business.

On David Susman's arrival in October 1952 he basically found the company to be without direction in that Richard Sonnenberg was recovering from a series of nervous breakdowns. Richard Sonnenberg was primarily an accountant with little interest in merchandise while his right hand man, Fred Kossuth was more interested in cutting costs rather than cut profit margins. There was an attempt to introduce the M&S stock counting and ordering systems but there was very little commitment with the exception of one or two executives, one of whom was another legend in the company, Ernst Loebenberg. Ernst. was one of Elie Susman's key men in Johannesburg and was passionate in the drive to introduce the implementation of M&S philosophies and methods. The drive was mostly resisted by the belief that "it may work in M&S but it won't work here". The lack of the exploitation of the advantages offered by M&S to strengthen key faster moving textile products and not using the quota to import some of their merchandise resulted in the counters being clogged with slower moving hard goods.

Ernst Loebenberg was an absolute icon in the company whose memorial today is fitting in the form of the current auditorium in Head office being named after him.

Born in 1920, he lived through the Great Depression and then fleeing Germany and the Nazi regime, he arrived in South Africa as a young Jewish teenager.

He would scour the stores of Woolworths. I remember well his visits to stores with an entourage of followers who struck fear into store staff when the designated white glove holder wiped above the fridges and even in railings of the sliding doors and lo behold if there was any dust. The departmental managers were expected to know each style number off by heart and the weekly sales thereof as he led you around your counter with his fatherly arm draped around your shoulder or holding your arm while he interrogated you but, in the end, no one was left without a greeting and a message of inspiration.

He was the main driver of the new generation of stores in the seventies in the form of Adderley street, Eastgate and Sandton and all those that followed as well as the erection of the current head office in the Mayor's garden across the road from the original head office. No comment about Ernst Loebenberg can go on without mention of his legendry "yellow perils". All his memos were on yellow paper and receipt of one immediately injected a sense of urgency into the recipient.

At the same time David Susman saw the need to establish similar M&S relationships and ethics with local suppliers and above all spread the gospel of St Michael which was to have "No compromise on quality standards, tight controls of stock levels and ruthless slaughtering of slow sellers"

It took about four years of hard work by David and his team to turn Woolworths around in terms of profit and a more healthy share value. Recognition of his success was rewarded in the form of David Susman being appointed to the board of directors of M&S which lasted about thirty years. The main advantage was during his regular visits to Baker street he was privy to the latest thinking of M&S and Woolworths had privileged access to M&S suppliers but mostly the greatest benefit was the final cementing of the relationship between the two companies.

LIFE IN THE SHADOW OF MARKS AND SPENCER

Everything in Woolworths became the mirror image of that in Marks & Spencer and I was convinced that Woolies and M&S were interchangeable, all that was different was the sign over the door. Over the years as the relationship grew closer.

The stores reflected the same display equipment with respect to counters, first of which were walk in department related with a till or maybe two tills at a corner. Goods were displayed usually in colour and size groupings with filler stocks being stored in shelves below the displays. The new and best-selling product was always exhibited on the ends with bold ticketing.

 Typical walk in counters are reflected below

The walk in counters were soon replaced in the sixties to free standing units as were evident in Marks and Spencer where merchandise was displayed similarly to the walk in counters and the principle of takings per square metre was focused on as the sales that the product produced determined how much space the product demanded. A typical early free standing counter with decentralised pay points is displayed below

Together with the counters there were rails of merchandise which was displayed face out on T-bars which were usually three to a rail. Other types of rails included a triangular form of rail that were mostly utilised to feature promotional and new product. An example of such a rail is below

The key discipline of the rack displays supporting the ticket frames was that apart from the rails having be perfectly aligned, the ticket frames had to be completely straight. I never forget a wonderful story being related to me by Geoff Sonnenberg, our divisional executive at the time in the Cape about his visit to France and how impressed he was when visiting the Moulin Rouge how the dancing girls managed to get their legs perfectly lined up. The end of the endearing story was that is how he wanted to see my ticket frames which I thought was a sad end to a nice story!

The pay points would be decentralised and in the late sixties and early seventies a pay point would typically consist of a standalone unit with NCR tills powered by batteries which were recharged on a rotational basis. Many suits were ruined by the leaking acid of these batteries and the frustration that ensued when a battery went flat which was mostly when there were long queues of impatient customers.

The selling teams consisted of a mix of skills that are coordinated in such a way that the customer had a most satisfying shopping experience.

The team was spearheaded by the manager who was the head of the store. This position was maybe supported by an assistant officer and they would ensure that the overall co-ordination of all the roles would deliver the most efficient running of the operation. A classic structure that they managed consisted of commercial or departmental managers each of whom would be responsible for a segment of the store.

Their roles were focused on ensuring that the displays were constantly fully stocked and that were optimally positioned and displayed proportionately appropriate to the customer demand.

The principle of proportionate displays extended to the product groups and determined where the group would be positioned in the store. If, for example, that the store was dominant in children's wear, it would in all likelihood be that the children's wear group would be located at the most busy entrance and in principle the best performing departments would enjoy the position and space accordingly within the group.

A characteristic textile store layout would typically look as follows

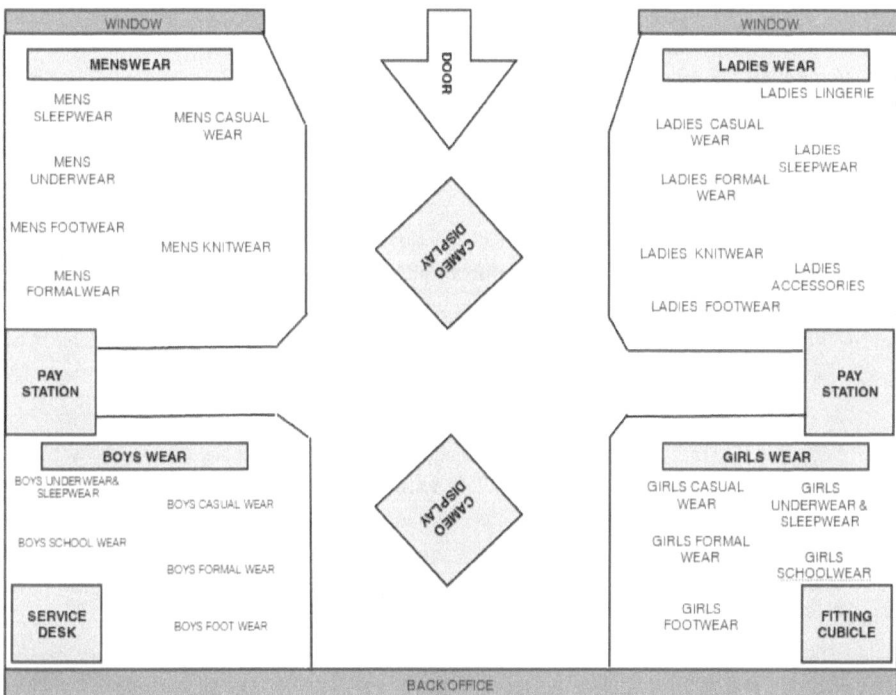

Food markets were pretty much standard in that the fridges were lined against the walls while ambient goods were packed on ordinary shelving. Meat markets were usually run on a concessionaire basis and therefore standards from one store to the next could be vastly different. Till checkouts would be at front of the market leading on to the clothing section.

In the mid-seventies the food markets were selling a mixture of product consisting of Marks & Spencer, some Woolworths product with the balance being that of independent brands. The very bold decision to eliminate the independent brands in their entirety was taken while I happened to be the food market manager at the Bloemfontein store. After the task of stripping all independent brands was completed, I recall with horror and surprise that we had more bare shelving than product. The customers were livid in that it meant that they were forced to duplicate their shopping habits as they had to now shop at other stores for their other favorite brands. Naturally the decline in turnover was horrific.

The fact that there were many gaps in the range placed immense pressure on the food technologists and buyers under the passionate guidance of Stephen Walker and Simon Susman, who had to actively collaborate with chosen suppliers to produce own brand product to Woolworth's specifications. Because the volumes were relatively small often the innovative development of new lines, many of which followed the M&S guidelines came with the agreement that Woolworths would have exclusivity of the product for an agreed period of time, for example six months, before the producer could introduce the product into their own range. An often-quoted example of the challenge to produce the Woolworth's volumes was that of yoghurts where the Woolworths orders did not even fill the supplier's pipes and the Woolworths product was produced in the test kitchens. The introduction of recipe dishes or readymade meals which were dominant M&S products was another classic illustration of market leading innovation.

It was in 1974 that Woolworths was the first retailer to introduce sell by dates and pre-prepare produce such as the washing of lettuce before delivering the produce to stores. The maintenance of the cold chain through the journey of the product from the supplier to a centralised storage and distribution centres before being placed on the refrigerated vehicles right to the store's fridge counter. Truth be known the strict maintenance of the cold chain was the reason as to why the freshness of Woolworths product such as milk out lasted that of their competitors. For a while certain product was delivered directly to the stores individually such as bananas but it was not long before all product was delivered through centralised distribution centres in Cape Town, Johannesburg and Durban. The haulage of the product was contracted out to specialists in this field. This philosophy gave a major competitive advantage over other chains who still had queues of sometimes substandard vehicles with no timeslot procedures at each store to deliver often high-risk product.

A feature of the early Woolworths stores was that the wall cladding was typically an especially coded "Woolworths" pink peg board which enabled flexibility to arrange hooks in equipment to maximise wall displays of merchandise. What was most common across all stores was that there was an absence of window displays and the windows were adorned with rack displays and not always displaying the newer and faster selling lines. The other notable feature was the variety of different signage mounted on store exteriors. There was no uniform logo signage adorning stores. The pink peg board was replaced in the early eighties by a new concept design named after the American contractor's company "Nexus". The fundamental difference was that it was dominated by a slatted strong dusty pink equipment design which in my opinion not only detracted from the merchandise, the inflexibility of the equipment restricted the innovative display methodologies. It was not surprising that the concept was relatively short lived and in the early nineties was replaced by what today is evident in most stores.

A hard to believe fact in terms of dress code in stores was that the sales assistants and supervisors wore identical designs and styles as those of their counterparts at Marks & Spencer. The management males were to wear suits only and never were allowed to remove their jackets often in some stores without air conditioning even when building a counter with a special issued tool or manoeuvring the buffer machine which often adopted a mind of its own and frequently ruined many a good suit. An interesting deviation from the dress code rules in stores was the fact that men were allowed only moustaches but no beards. The exception to this rule was for textile technologists. A textile technologist was an extremely rare breed and because at the time there was no formal training available in South Africa they were sourced from overseas and because of the scarcity they were allowed to have beards.

In head office the dress code was strictly suits only while women had to wear stockings. In 1984 there was a revolution which I am proud to say I was part of. In a motion agreed by all including the then Managing Director, Michael Stakol, it was decided to don on a particular day blazers and chino trousers. This bold move was met with shock and horror and a delegation was summoned to the office of David Susman and after some intense negotiation it was agreed that blazers and chinos would be allowed to be part of the dress code on Fridays only. In a way I believe it is sad that today's dress code is non-existent and my personal view is that pretty much anything goes and that t-shirts and shorts are disrespectful when dealing with suppliers and money values amounting to millions. Thankfully store attire is still disciplined.

In an attempt to attract the best retailing staff, Woolworths was the first of local retailers to introduce a pension fund, medical aid and maternity leave. Driven by David Susman who had the belief that all staff had to be properly fed in each store and Head Office had to be equipped with a fully equipped kitchen and dining room where hot meals were offered at immensely discounted prices, a practice that still exists today. As a young bachelor in my early days, this was my main meal of the day and was much appreciated.

Another point of note was the fact that at the height of the apartheid regime in the mid-seventies when the law was that staff ablution facilities had to be separate for whites and non-whites. In blatant defiance of the law of the land, David Susman instructed that in stores that the separation be disbanded and ablutions be shared by all regardless of colour.

Similarly jobs were provided to activists who were closely monitored by the authorities. Two such people were Peter Jones who was very close to Steve Biko who I worked with in the Somerset West store and another wonderful person who was my assistant for quite some time being Sheila Lapinski, an activist who suffered the constant attention of the security police. Coupled to this was the disbanding of management positions being reserved for whites only which for some presented uncomfortable situations of having to be managed by a non-white.

Probably the most notable similarity between Woolworths and M&S was the documentation and processes that were implemented in the counting, performance measurement, ordering and distribution of the merchandise to stores.

Prior to the advent of computerisation the pivotal document that lay at the centre of the systems was the checking list. The checking list administration was very much a manual system whereby the layout was laid out in the product groupings. Below is a simplified view of a checking list to assist the process understanding.

DEPARTMENT 148 shirts				WEEK ENDING	28-Feb						
STORE	333 DURBAN										
PRODUCT	MENS SHORT SLEEVE										
ITEM	DESCRIPTION	SELL PRICE	COLOUR /SIZE	UNITS OPEN STOCK	RANDS CLOSE STOCK	ON ORDER	UNITS SALES	RANDS SALES	LOC 1	LOC 2	LOC 3
12345	Check 2 pocket	9.99	Red	200	100	0	100	1000	10	60	30
12346	Check 1 pocket	9.99	Blue	500	300	600	200	2000	150	80	70
12347	Stripes	9.99	White	400	100	300	300	3000	30	20	50
TOTAL				1100	500	900	600	6000	190	160	150
13456	White Basic	7.99	small	300	100	0	200	1598	30	20	50
		7.99	medium	500	200	0	300	2397	60	40	100
		7.99	large	400	100	0	300	2397	10	30	60
TOTAL				1200	400	0	800	6392	100	90	210

The process commenced by the physical counting as per the layout of the checking list which was pre-printed by the department with the catalogue on a sheet which was slightly larger than an A3 size. Each department was counted and processed bi-weekly.

The designated counter was usually the sales assistant responsible for that particular department where stock may exist at different locations such as the stock room, floor displays and other feature displays. Once the physical count was completed the count sheet went to the general office where the units were manually converted to the monetary value through the loud pounding of adding machines. The stock in transit values were added by referring to the outstanding on order delivery instructions which were clipped to a board for each department and were hanging on a fixture usually in the stock room.

Photo copying machines were a scarce commodity up until the mid-eighties and if the store was lucky enough to have one it was usually housed in the manager's office and only authorised users who would have had appropriate training would be allowed to use them. In the main carbon paper was inserted in between the sheets and the figures were copied over the master to produce the original for the store, a copy for head office distribution department and a central merchandising department copy. This was a tedious task as the pressure using a sturdy pen was required to ensure clear copies were generated. As per the example in the diagram certain lines were selected on a rotational basis to have grid count by colour and size in order that the distribution department to complete a build back exercise to the original percentage size ratio bought. The central merchandising department which had a team of data capturers would collate all the stores figures and generate a national summary. The merchandiser would utilize this information to compile a completed document that included the stock values that were in transit to the stores, the value of physical stock and the balance of unmade orders at suppliers. This document would be hand delivered to the printing department in the basement under the strict supervision of Mr. Geoff Higgens, who was for some reason feared by all, where the document was typeset and printed and distributed through the mailing system to all the many relevant recipients. Coupled to this document the merchandiser prepared what was known as a standstill document which in essence compared the actuals to that what was planned.

The planning part was that what was done in the production book. Simply described the individual items each had a page which was broken down into weeks and summarised to months. The budget sales for the season for the product was split across the weeks in a shape that was largely determined by historical sales. The planned stocks in stores was determined by six weeks forward planned sales, a further two weeks allowance for that in transit to stores and four week value of stock to be held at the manufacturer and the intake plan required to meet the target which ultimately represented the suppliers production programme. Each blue page was totalled through to a yellow summary page for each category and finally through to the first page for the total department.

The start points of analysing and comparing the actual performance to the intended plan at a point in time, is to firstly to compare actual sales to date at total departmental level and drill down to product level and based on the result, review the planned sales for the balance of the season.

The potential new sales forecast is then compared to the actual commitment of product in the form of stock on hand at stores, product in transit and that at the supplier as well as the orders in the pipeline to determine the resultant shortage or surplus of stock.

In the scenarios below the assumption is that the department consists of a product which is over performing, another that is under performing and one that is selling to expectation.

The procedure which needs to be followed can be broken down into three distinct activities.

- The recording of the total plan for the season in terms of sales and the planned breaking stocks at the end of the season as well as the current week's performance which has just been completed.
- Based on the comparison of the actual sales to date in relation to that which was budgeted for may require a review of the balance of sales to be achieved and thereby create a revised forecast for the total season. The change in the sales forecast may also then require an adaptation of the planned breaking stocks to reflect the reality of the sales plan.
- Once the realistic revised sales performance has been established, the result then needs to be compared to the total stock commitment and assessed whether there is sufficient stock in the pipeline to achieve the revised targets. If this is not the case, a plan has to be devised in order to determine what action is required to achieve this or conversely there may be a consequent surplus of stock which will have to be reduced.

Diagrammatically this can be illustrated as follows

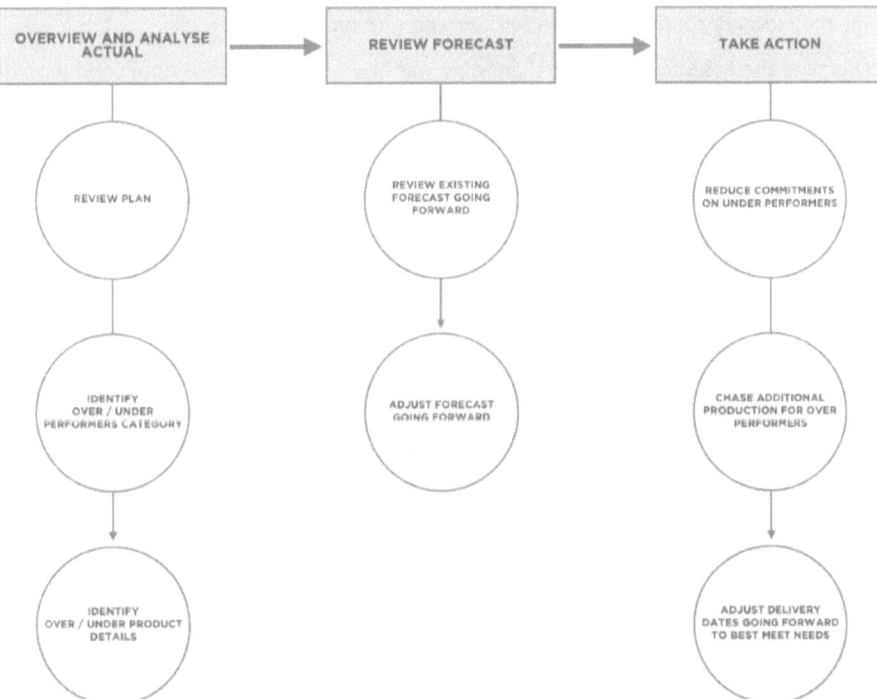

The analysis and review took place in a weekly meeting with the head of the merchandise group and was usually a tense affair where the team lived and died by the performance of their department and suffered severe consequences for any hint of non-compliance in meeting targets.

What was fascinating of this era was the fact that 90% of the focus was on turnover and the % performance on the previous year. There was not much reference to any other key performance indicators such as margins or gross or net profit at group level let alone at departmental level as it is prevalent in today's world where turnover is seen as pure vanity while the key measures are profits and cash in the bank.

In the world today the pointers are vastly different, as stakeholders need to be able to check whether the performance is on track to achieve the strategic planning objectives which are measured against a suite of pre-set performance indicators. The most common performance pointers which are assigned targets that will deliver the desired financial requirements, are the following.

    Sales
    Markdowns
    Buying margin
    Sales margin
    Stock forward cover
    Stock annual turn
    Return on inventory investment

It is absolutely imperative that these indicators are clearly understood by all members of the retail team both in the head office and stores and what role they play in the support of them. The measures are almost always referred to in financial reports as shareholders utilise these to determine their level of confidence in the company performance.

Upon reflection, the M&S model of merchandising was in essence relatively simple and determined basically the amount of intake required at key points in time. Diagrammatically this can be modestly described as follows

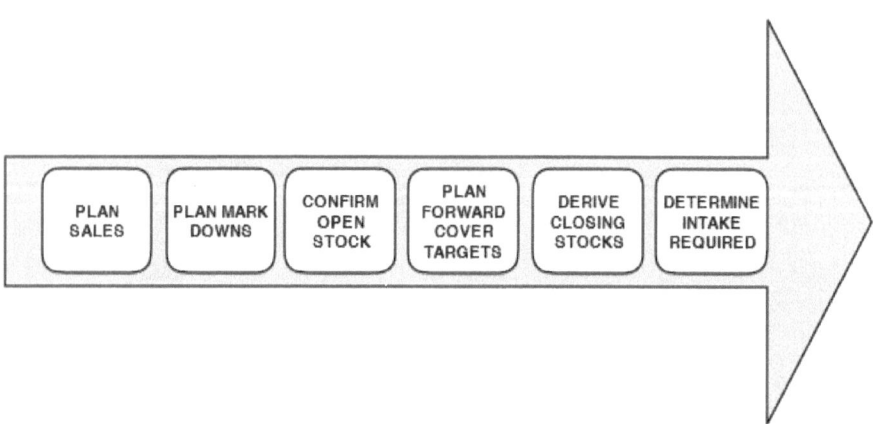

Even the buying process was relatively simple. It was up to the merchandiser to produce an intake plan from a departmental line summary which would have been formulated as part of the team. At the time there was no design or trend team because the bulk of the range was inspired by the Marks and Spencer ranges which because of seasonal difference South Africa could benefit from cherry picking the best performers of the season which preceded that of South Africa. The other main source was from innovative suppliers who presented ranges to the buyers and their task was simply to fill their shopping list which in essence was the intake plan provided by the merchandiser. The quantities were largely determined by the store catalogue and was usually relatively static dependent on the number of units required to fill a display and a quantity required for back up. So close was the processes of M&S followed, the quantities ordered were in dozens in spite of South Africa being decimalized. In many cases, particularly those suppliers which were 100% Woolworths very often dictated the selection of product. A classic example would be that of Bibette who were part of the Seardell group. They supplied in the main ladies fashions. The two key drivers strengthened the domination was the fact that Michael Stakol, the Managing Director at the time being the late seventies and in the eighties had a very close relationship with Aaron Searll, the chairman of Seardell and Kenny Winer, the Managing director of Bibette. Because of this, the departments were committed to fill the capacity as dictated by the plant irrespective of the merits of the product. Having said this, they were a very innovative and energetic in the sense they would on their own initiative manufacture as an example twenty four garments without even notifying the department and deliver these either to the Claremont or Adderley street store on a Friday. Should the weekend sales be good it was usually followed up with full orders on instruction. The costing system was also quite unique. The first point was that there was very little opportunity for negotiation. Because the departments were structured by a rigid price point grouping base the process was simply that the entire range was displayed and irrespective of what the actual cost price a panel would decide on the apparent value that each garment represented. The panel consisted both of supplier and Woolworths who would the select the appropriate price point that would be contracted. In theory there may be a garment based on costing would qualify for a 9.99 home but it's comparative value may determine that it lives in the 12.99 range. Naturally this made for Bibette to be a highly profitable manufacturing plant in Seardell group.

Similar relationships were formed with medium to small manufacturers, many of which were family owned, as per the philosophy of M&S. In the Lingerie department small and medium suppliers such as Lolita (Rosenbergs), Val Hau (Chaitmans), Baywear knitting (Helliwells), Suzi (Lipworths), Riviera Fashions (Berrils) products were quite prevalent. While the main benefit was that there was strict control over quality and guaranteed availability of production capacity there was not much innovation and the buying department simply provided samples (more often than not M&S garments) to fill the capacity. Usually an exception to the rule were extremely innovative, such as Suzi products which made the buyer's job much easier and the factory grew substantially.

Large quantities of fabric, usually woven, particularly yarn dyes which have longer lead times as the design needs to be specified would be purchased by Woolworths from both local and off shore mills to be held in storage and because the meterage volumes can be an important factor in negotiating keener prices. These fabrics are then allocated to mostly smaller cut, make and trim suppliers who then only quote for in the main the labour cost and after giving a rating of the fabric usage will be issued the fabric and trims may be purchased by either the supplier or Woolworths. The downside of this process was that there may be substantial unused fabric which may not be on trend for future seasons or would be forced into garments which resulted in a higher cost of write down in garment form. Change in buying roles can lead to a reluctance to use leftover fabrics as if resultant sales are poor they would reflect on the new buyer's assessments.

A very few vertical suppliers were utilized, a prime example being Meritex who manufactured knitted fabrics, dyed them and made up the garments such as underwear and some outerwear such as t shirts in reasonably large volumes.

Tailoring was in the main done by specialist suppliers such as Rex Trueform and Monatic.

Trial quantities of product, especially knitwear were imported from M&S in their current season and sent to a selected number of stores in order to get a reading for the upcoming season in South Africa. If the results were favourable a full quantity could be imported or manufactured locally.

EARLY COMPUTERISATION

In the mid-sixties under the guidance of Frans Wimmers, Woolworths was a forerunner in the introduction of the age of computerisation. Although it was well before my time, I am led to believe that these were very large machines which probably had as much power as an average smart phone in today's day and age. A fundamental error was that the department that was selected as the trial was the bras and corsetry department, which because of the number of permutations of sizes and cup variations made this a very complex excercise through the use of cardboard kimble tags which were attached to each garment and after the sale these were removed from the garment to be collected and be sent to the head office for data capturing.

The kimble tag was the forerunner of barcodes that was used mostly in the retail fashion industry in order to control stocks, deduce sales and aid the distribution that included machine readable data that supported punch card processing. The real downside was however the physical collection of all the tags as many did not reach the point of data capture. The net effect of this was the distortion of information which resulted in the fact that the results could not be trusted and eventually the whole project was disbanded.

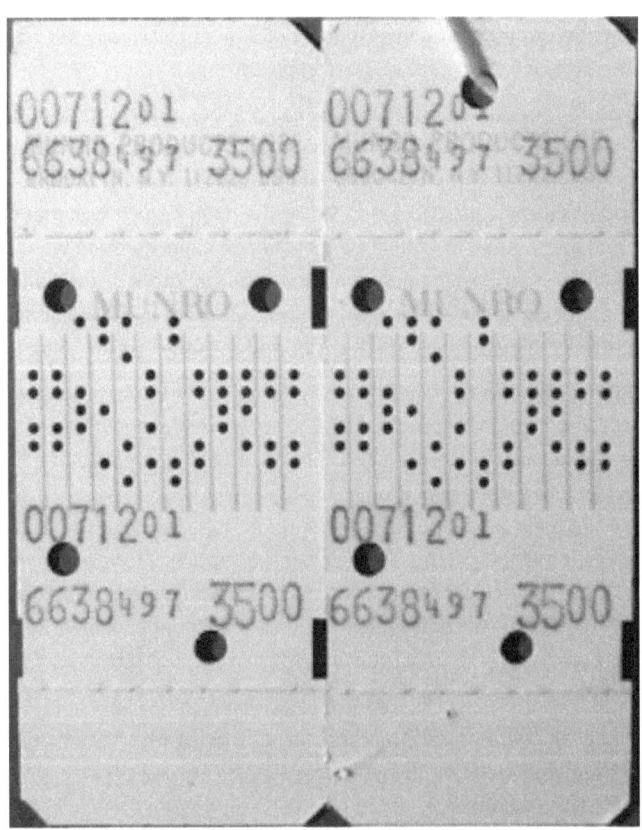

An example of the kimble tag is illustrated above

Marks & Spencer were also wary of computerization and hence like Woolworths were relatively late in joining the age of computerised systems.

It was therefore not surprising that while the rest of the retailing world were advancing into sophisticated systems development and the general use of the personal computer it was only in 1984 that the first PC was introduced into Woolworths. I know this because I was the first lucky incumbent to receive an IBM 5150 Personal Computer and a box of Lotus 123 software which was predecessor to other spreadsheet packages and today's most widely used Microsoft Excel. It was exciting times and after studying the manual intensely, I developed the first production programmes and progressed to a number of other tools that made life much easier. It was not long before more and more machines were introduced and in comparison, to today's options were very slow and with restricted capacity.

IBM 5150 Personal Computer

The use of the floppy disc had the Lotus 123 systems disc in the one drive with the data disc inserted into the other. As the number of users increased, security became an issue and a manager was appointed to control the booming IT department and the discs had to be stored overnight in safes. Floppy discs have long been obsolete.

Early Foods systems were extremely basic and was limited to the main system which was the transfer of picking orders from the office to the distribution centres. The orders were prepared manually by the merchandisers often just by gut feel and handed over to a data capture person who would have to enter the orders in order to transmit them down a telephone line to the distribution centre where there were usually only two receipt points.

The process was cumbersome and the transmission was very slow. When I think back to the way the distribution centre received orders I recall the vision of the data capturer frantically keying in the orders and then pressing the send button. She would then pick up her knitting and do a few rows while the information trundled down the phone line for about five minutes prior to completion.

A revolution in the mid-eighties was the introduction of fax machines at suppliers for them to send in the availabilities more easily rather than spending ages on the phone. When this was first introduced there was great resistance from the suppliers, particularly the farmers having to invest in such advanced equipment.

ORGANISATIONAL STRUCTURES
Like M&S the organisational structure in Woolworths was virtually the mirror image across all of the three main disciplines being Clothing, Foods and Stores and the hierarchy levels were also very similar.

In stores the region was controlled by a Divisional Executive while stores were managed by a Store Manager assisted by an Assistant Manager and then supported by a team of Department Managers who looked after the key categories such as Ladieswear, Menswear, Foods, etc.

In Head Office the structures too were almost no different as that applied at M&S. The organisational clothing structure with the key functional posts started at Company level where the CEO and directors were responsible then cascading down to the group executives who were in control of each category group. Within each group were sub groups that were managed by category managers and the departments resided in each sub group with Buyers, Merchandisers and Location planners or distributors functioning at these levels.

It should be noted that in the illustration the designation of the location planner who was housed as part of the relevant department is the alternative option to the distributor who may well be part of the centralised distribution department which consisted of a team of distributors who may be responsible for a number of departments. I have my own view of the pros and cons of the two options.

Some organisational structures do differentiate the allocation function between the merchandiser who focuses on the forecasting and production planning at the higher level and that of the allocator or location planner who is responsible to distribute the product to the stores in the most appropriate combinations of styles, colour and sizes which met the store profiles. The benefits of such a centralised structure is that there could be a cost saving advantage especially where smaller departments do not warrant a dedicated staff member but added to this is a pool of knowledge which develops a highly skilled team who are able to cross pollinate information, coordinate inter departmental promotions effectively and develop consistent techniques and skills. The identification of common emerging trends contributed to the optimisation of sales and assist in the control of stock quantities at a very detailed level and thereby maximise profits. Close connections to the departmental merchandisers were maintained to ensure that their actions were aligned to the departmental strategy and plans.

Initially the supporting roles such as technology and marketing were set apart from the buying groups. It must be noted that the role of the technologist was spread quite widely mainly due to the scarcity of resources in South Africa while the Marketing department was virtually nonexistent as like M&S, the philosophy was that there was no need to advertise as word of mouth and trusted reliability was sufficient to effectively promote the business and evade perceived unnecessary overheads.

The Foods group structure followed more or less the same framework with the exception that while the role names were the same, the functional operations differed dramatically. Merchandisers were responsible to focus on the placement of orders and it has to be said that this was not very scientifically done, with guesswork and gutfeel being the main driver in the placement of orders with the relevant suppliers which were delivered in bulk to the distribution centres. The distributor than provided the picking instructions to the distribution centres in order to allocate to the individual stores. This function too was also not too scientific and depended mainly on the historical track record of each individual store.

Buyers in the Foods group were predominantly responsible for the packaging design and the product mix across the range whereas the development and quality control of the products sat squarely on the shoulders of the highly trained technologists.

One of the greatest assets of Woolworths, like M&S, was the focus on training. The common requirements of each role were that there was a structured methodology of training which included on the job training where the incumbent was mentored by a qualified and experienced more senior specialist who in turn had exposure to effective training methods and performance management techniques. Ideally as the trainee progressed, they took on the responsibility for a small section of their department in order to gain the confidence and skills that stood them in good stead going forward and also served as a contingency in the event of the loss of senior personnel.

Coupled to on the job training was the formal classroom style lecturing as was necessary and was performed by either internal or external tutors who provided the theory that is matched to that which has been learnt on the job. This was of great importance as it is not uncommon that with on the job training exclusively was the fact that the poor habits of the trainer are frequently transferred downwards.

Equally important is for new appointees to have an understanding and appreciation of the roles of their counterparts in other areas of the business. In order for this to be achieved they spent adequate time attached to specialists in other fields. An example would be where a buyer in training would need to spend time in stores interacting with customers, at suppliers, with merchandisers, technologists, the marketing team and packaging specialists, in the warehouse and with the logistical experts including forwarding agents. These attachments were well thought out with specific objectives in mind and were followed up in formal reviews in front of a panel of experts from each area who test their understanding.

In summary, the business was run in a very copycat fashion which unfortunately at times restricted innovation and the application of general performance indicators. This made for quite a simple process and provided a very secure paternal environment until the next era arrived when the merger with Truworths and Topics took place.

THE MERGER AND CREATION OF WOOLTRU
The Truworths business started as the Alliance Trading Company in 1917 which went on to become Truworths in the 1930's. In the 1940's they started their own manufacturing base in South Africa in the seventies consisted only of Bonwit which was eventually gobbled up by the Seardell group. Truworths introduced credit in the 1950's. Prior to the merger, the story goes that Leonard Shawzin who was part of the founding family and its subsidiaries requested David Susman if Woolworths

would consider taking over his business as none of his family had any interest in continuing with the company.

As a result the merger took place in 1981 and the Wooltru group was formed. The Group consisted of Woolworths, a pure cash business with predominantly basic merchandise, Truworths which focused on the high end of fashion and traded heavily on an account based system. Topics was a smaller chain of middle of the road merchandise while a very small chain Top Centre concentrated exclusively on the black market. Included in the bundle was the stationery chain CNA and the computer support business which eventually became a separate entity known as Wooltru computer services which had an extensive data capture section and main frame system that catered in the main for the accounts systems of chiefly Truworths and Topics.

Over a twenty-year relationship the company underwent much change and transformation that significantly improved sales and profits, before it was unbundled from the group in 1997.

The change over brought with it a major revolution to specifically the character of Woolworths. Up until the merger Woolworths remained a conservative cost-conscious business with significant cash reserves. The Wooltru group initially was headed up by Tony Williamson who commenced with a merging of the organisational structures through the swapping of some key resources. The most notable change was the shift of Eddie Parfitt from the Woolworths directorate to Truworths as Managing Director. Woolworths gained the talents of Brian Frost from the Truworths Zimbabwe stable who headed up the Store Operations group of Woolworths, Neil Balfour moved into an executive position in the Foods Group from Topics and Christo Barnard was transferred from Truworths to head up the Wooltru computer services.

The most impactful change to Woolworths was the appointment of Stuart Campbell from Truworths who was tasked to asses and recommend the change to the organisational structure in such a way that it would transform Woolworths into a much more dynamic, less paternal and not as top-heavy organisation.

This assignment commenced with an extensive organisational survey conducted throughout the company which was the first hint of major restructures in the offing and for the first time in Woolworths there was an air of insecurity amongst all staff. This came to be true with a meaningful trimming of numbers at all levels of staff, mostly in stores which was done quite brutally and for me changed the culture of the company. Geoff Sonnenberg, executive and grandchild of the founder forcefully emphasized this point during his retirement speech where he publicly attacked the unsympathetic approach of Stuart Campbell and the fact that he was ruining people's lives. I often wonder what went through the mind of his best friend David Susman who was part of the audience.

THE MAYOR'S GARDEN
Logistically the largest challenge was the accommodation of all the facets of the group in a centralised location. Construction of a new state of the art building commenced in 1984 in what was known as the Mayor's Garden which was directly behind the City Hall and across the road from the existing Woolworths Head office. The land was procured from the City Council on a ninety-nine-year lease agreement and the cost was estimated to be a whopping forty million rand. Interestingly the project was headed up by none other than the legend Ernst Loebenberg.

Wooltru House

The design was quite unique in that part of the provision was that a certain percentage of the ground level had to be retained which was satisfied through a central atrium being bordered by six floor levels in a circular fashion. The other proviso was that the height of the building was determined by the fact that the building could not obscure the view of Table Mountain from the parade which is the reason why it was restricted to six floors.

Initially the Wooltru Computer services occupied the first floor consisting mainly of the data capture staff with access to the main frame computers which were securely housed in the basement. Also, at this level on the other side was the Auditorium and presentation rooms with a dining room and catering facilities below. The upper six floors were utilised by the main players being Truworths, Woolworths, Topics and the top floor accommodated the executive suites. Topics only spent a brief period in the building, sharing a floor with Truworths before relocating to the Golden Acre.

The Wooltru Head Office occupied a beautiful charming historical building diagonally across the road on the corner of Spin and Corporation streets

By this time the small Top Centre chain had been disbanded and the specialised buying function for the black market was transferred into Woolworths headed by David Blend. This too was eventually absorbed into the Woolworths parent departments. CNA also remained independent until it too was eventually sold off to the Edcon group.

THE IMPACT OF THE MERGER ON WOOLWORTHS
If truth be known in hindsight, preceding the merger, Woolworths was in a phase of complacency apart from the development of the store infrastructure. Major flagship stores were opened in new mall type shopping centres that were springing up particularly in the north where beautiful shops such as Eastgate, Sandton, Rosebank and the like evolved. Other than that, life simply trundled on in the same way it had for a number of years. There were no innovative system developments and the

ranges were very much the same season in and season out guided by the M&S strategies and any deviation was strongly resisted.

For me, a classic example of this was when I was in the Ladies Underwear department, I mocked up a triple pack of bikinis in a bra box and made a proposal of a multi pack of panties to go into stores. This turned out to be much more difficult than I had envisioned. After some intense motivation to the relevant executive and director of the group, I found myself in the office of a senior director Robbie Stern, a grandson of the founder, to present the concept. It was in no uncertain terms that he disparaged me and my hair brained idea and out rightly rejected the proposal. Unperturbed, I proceeded to get over stickers for the bra box and packed panties in them and clandestinely sent modest quantities to a few stores. To put it bluntly, the result was that they flew off the shelves and was considered a huge success. It was not long thereafter that whatever could go in a box in the form of a multi pack was pursued to the extent that it was almost ludicrous.

The two organisations were definitely not a perfect fit. Woolworths was enormously conservative, cost conscious to the extreme and heavily reliant on the M&S philosophies. Truworths and Topics, on the other hand were retail street fighters and remained not averse to risk taking. They depended largely on the account-based model, offering leading edge fashion ranges and were probably the most advanced in systems development to handle the accounts as well as the merchandising and buying applications.

The arrival of the new compatriots brought a sense of urgency and an appreciation of the potential benefits of such a relationship. Apart from the wakeup call that the revised organisation structures that Stuart Campbell introduced the next logical step was the benefit of having sophisticated computer infrastructure on hand.

It was thus decided to embark on a new initiative in order to best utilise this facility. The decision was a very controversial one as it flew in the face of the philosophies of M&S who were anti automation as well as the bloody nose that Woolworths experienced in the sixties and seventies after their venture into stock controls in the form of Kimble tags.

Without being privy to the political battles that raged behind closed doors, I was withdrawn from my normal job and was tasked to prepare an exhibition of the buying and merchandising paper trails in the clothing arena. While it was a large complex exercise, I completed the presentation which took the form of every single document being pasted on the walls of a room and the relationship of each manuscript being linked to each other. It was only on the day of the presentation that I realised the seriousness of the process to reach the decision. I found myself surrounded by the most senior representatives in the company and others, but more importantly the tension could be cut with a knife. The audience all listened intently with little comment as I walked them through the exposition. It was only after the completion that an emotive discussion erupted with regard to the practicality, the integrity and the impact of such a major change to enter the unexplored world of automation. The final conclusion was that Woolworths would embark on becoming part of the computerisation age.

Apart from the sharing of the common computer services, the individual companies continued as separate entities for a number of years in spite of the fact that the same building and facilities were shared. The intermingling of staff from the different companies was discouraged until the late eighties when the Truworths House was erected on the site of the old Woolworths head office and Wooltru House then became Woolworths House. Topics was sold off and has since been joined the graveyard of past retailers.

In 1997 the Wooltru Group was unbundled and Woolworths and Truworths were listed as separate companies on the JSE.

LEADERSHIP ERAS

During the period up until the unbundling, Woolworths went through a number of what can be described as leadership eras. The one thread of uniformity through these eras was the fact that the culture of offering good values with a high commitment to the maintenance of the best quality standards and the product returns policy while fostering customer relationships to be kept to maximum remained an important priority.

Under the chairmanship of David Susman during the seventies and eighties there was an era where the board of directors consisted of a relatively young breed of entrepreneurs where directors such as Michael Stakol, who was appointed Managing Director at the age of thirty four while the other board members and executives such as David Glasser, Stephen Walker, Michael Wolffe, Dave Collie, Steven Mervis, the secretary of the company Syd Muller, the head of human resources led by John Spinks and Andrew Wilson as well as Eddie Parfett were all in their mid-thirties which made for an energetic, competitive and dynamic leadership team which was underpinned by an enthusiastic bunch of aspirant executives.

Micael Stakol (*1970 – 1987*) was a colourful character with an air of arrogance but was most of all a true merchant. He was a risk taker and ruthless in his dealings. Product reviews were anxious affairs and it was not uncommon for tears to flow and the berating of all levels was often the order of the day. While he had technically the overall responsibility for foods, he seldom became involved in day to day management except when the head like Stephen Walker or Simon Susman were away and he would march into the group and we would be ordered to launch the most aggressive promotions in massive volumes that were seldom heard of. What he is well remembered for was his denim purchases. At the time in the early eighties, Woolworths had a strict policy that denim would not be part of the ranges due to the poor colourfastness of the fabric. During an overseas trip Michael Stakol disregarded this policy and bought a shed load of denim. Being part of Ladieswear at the time, I recall visiting the Woolworths warehouse in Paarden Eiland which was ably run by Bardie Badenhorst who was totally distraught as the warehouse was packed with denim to the ceiling. We made almost every product type in denim such as skirts, jumpsuits, trousers, shorts and I am sure if we could we would have made ladies underwear in denim in order to eat it all up. As a result, we were inundated with customer complaints who had white couches that they suffered the effects of blue colour transfer from the denim garments.

As mentioned before, Michael had special relationships with chosen suppliers. It was while I was in the Ladies Dress department where we had a particularly mediocre 100% supplier who openly admitted to me, standing next to his Rolls Royce, that the factory was simply a hobby for his wife. He, however enjoyed the support of Michael Stakol whom he advised on investments and that his main source of wealth was from elsewhere. I was instructed by the then Group Head at the time to inform them that we were going to cease business. This task was a particularly unpleasant and fiery and an experience I will not easily forget. Safe to say two days later, I was summoned to my Group Head's office where I was informed that we would be continuing business with the supplier and to not question the reasons why.

There is no doubt that similar relationships continued to exist with suppliers and agents. Another experience that I had was when we had booked our entire season's yarn dye fabric after intense selection of colour combinations and meterage with one agent and all was done and dusted when the agent called a meeting. He put it simply by saying that the indents were to be transferred to a competitor of his who represented the same yarn dye house. He would not elaborate as to the reasons why.

So sadly, Michael Stakol eventually fell on his sword in the early nineties amidst some allegations that he enjoyed a cut of commissions of orders placed with certain agents and he exited the business overnight.

Syd Muller, (*1987-2000*) the Company Secretary at the time took over the leadership. He was a wonderful businessman, but one downfall was his understanding of the merchandise compositions and there was a challenging period trying to read the reigning fashion trends correctly. Unfortunately, this led to a period where Woolworths lost the plot in terms of satisfying the customers wants and performed poorly. Syd was loved by his people but there was a depressing change during this time and the quip in the corridors was "the beatings will continue until the morale improves". While the Wooltru board tolerated the lack lustre performance for a while, the early nineties brought some dramatic modification.

Syd Muller continued as the executive chairman of Woolworths until he resigned his executive position and directorships within Woolworths Holdings in order to take up a chief executive position in a new company to be formed within the Wooltru group to focus on Wooltru's new electronic commerce initiative.

The change came in the form of the first external appointment of Farrel Ratner (*1992- 2000*) who was head hunted from Edgars where he was renowned as the Menswear director. The package was quite significant, and it is believed that he was offered a six-figure lump sum just to accept the offer. He also came under certain conditions, one being that he bring with him Edgars head of Marketing, Carol Grolman who would create a marketing division at Woolworths.

Farrel Ratner arrived with a bang and quickly started shaking things up. He carried a similar attitude of arrogance as that of Michael Stakol, was also a true merchant and was absolutely passionate about the product. Store visits were often a side show where he was always accompanied by a large entourage. Often customers stood in awe as this relatively short man ranted and raved over issues surrounded by a downcast group of people while he rebuked and belittled them. I will never forget during a visit to Adderley Street store where he said loudly that we are all so pathetic that he could not believe that while he was at Edgars they were scared of us.

It was no different in Head Office and in particular during his product reviews which were attended by everyone except the cleaning ladies, he seemed to enjoy playing to the gallery. Sadly, his remarks and comments were often personal and sometimes defamatory much to the amusement of his broad audience. I also, while in the men's shirts department came to be the target of his wrath. Together with my buying colleague we were in the process of presenting the forthcoming season's range and the collar shapes of white shirts was being debated where the basic subsidised white shirt was sold at a discounted price because of the volumes while the identical fashion white shirt except it sported longer pointed collars were sold at a premium because of the fashion trend and the category in which they were housed. While his point that we were being unfair to the customer was probably correct he became so infuriated that he threw his bottle of water at us which hit me and bounced off into the face of my then boss. No apology was ever received either directly or indirectly. Similarly, when he was reviewing a range and the garments, he considered to be substandard "dreg" he would unceremoniously remove garments from the display frames and throw them on the floor which naturally was a bitter pill to swallow for the team that was presenting. I never could understand the fact that this gentleman who seemed to derive such pleasure from exerting his power actually hated delivering formal speeches.

Supplier visits were also conducted in a similar vain with groups of relevant participants and one could not but help feeling sorry for the suppliers who lived in fear of such events. Often almost impossible demands were imposed on the merchants accompanied with veiled threats as to what the consequences may be should there be noncompliance to any requests.

Simon Susman joined Woolworths in 1982 after working at Marks & Spencer in London, where he was the executive professional assistant to the chairman, Marcus Sieff.

Susman headed the retail operations and the food and clothing divisions of Woolworths and was appointed to the board in 1995. He became chief executive in 2000.

Under his leadership Woolworths entered the convenience food store format in a joint venture with a fuel retailer. At the time, this was a bold strategic decision and has since been imitated by its competitors.

It was under his direction that Woolworths won the internationally respected responsible retailer of the year award from the World Retail Congress in 2008 in recognition of its business practices, known as the good business journey.

In the late nineties Simon Susman moved from the Foods Group and swopped roles with Brian Frost who headed up the Store Operations group for a while before moving onto the clothing area for more exposure. It was only natural that in 2000 the company was divided into two distinct areas where Simon Susman took accountability for the Woolworths chain, including procurement, supply, retail, marketing, finance and human resources, while Brian Frost became responsible for Woolworths channel activities, comprising information technology, logistics and financial services.

Farrel Ratner decided to resign and take on a consultancy role as procurement advisor to Woolworths.

While I was working under Simon Susman in the Foods group, I learnt it was very clear that his greatest attribute was his passion for the product and his closeness to the work on the ground. My experience in foods was that he spent probably half of his time on the work floor getting intricately involved in the technology, tasting and giving input into the development of ranges together with the teams and suppliers with whom he built some wonderful relationships. Simon had an absolute love for stores and was the darling of store management including the sales teams right down to the shelf packers.

While as the CEO, his responsibilities distanced himself from the product detail he remained passionate and every Saturday saw him roaming the peninsula visiting stores and pleasantly interacting with the staff and customers. Simon was a firm believer in that the bulk of decisions originate from the stores and customer and his frequent quote was "the truth about the business is in the stores.

Even as head of foods he really tried to grow the business by attracting outside talent, even though sometimes not that successful, in the hope that they would take the business to newer heights. This strategy continued as he assumed the role of CEO overlooking the entire business.

This strategy was so impactful that I have created a separate section for this topic.

RESOURCING OVERSEAS AND EXTERNAL LOCAL LEADERSHIP/MANAGEMENT

Before I embark on the detail of the recruitment of world class talent and local expert with the sole purpose to keep Woolworths relevant. Prior to the influx of external appointees, there was in the earlier days a very strict policy influenced by the philosophies of M&S where at whatever level of education you possessed the initiation consisted of spending a significant period of time in stores. In my particular case, after completing a degree in commerce, the first and only job I was offered in Woolworths was that of trainee manager and hope that would climb the career ladder from the bottom. Thus I started in the receiving bay and stockroom and eventually progressed to the sales floor and took on responsibility for a departmental area. Progression over the next three years took me to about five stores including being far from home in Bloemfontein which was a traumatic experience for a young beach bum being sent inland. Eventually I returned to Cape Town to the brand new flagship Adderley street store before I was considered to be suitable for recruitment into Head Office. It was a slow process until the day arrived where staff were accepted directly into Head office without store experience and were not culture brainwashed as a true 'Woolies' employee.

I believe overall the impact of the influx of such overseas and external local leadership and experts was not necessarily a positive strategy for the company. In most cases I think that the company suffered as a result.

Broadly there is a common theme that exists in that such external incumbents come at a price with high expectations. Many come from different backgrounds and experiences with very little knowledge of or commitment to the Woolworths corporate culture.

The most important goal is that there is the need to assert themselves in a short period of time and more often than not, achieve this by making changes that are not necessarily in the best interests of the company. With the focus being mainly on the set down personal performance goals the key attributes of retailing can easily be neglected, such as the complete dedication to the principles of unnegotiable standards of quality, the understanding of the profiles of South African Woolworths customers and the pillar of consistent availability of goods and the maintenance of the best possible values at acceptable margins. To me the slow or virtually no growth of internal talented resources did not only break down the continuity of the core Woolworths principles but also frequently the morale and aspirations of many home grown Woolworths aspirants were left in tatters. Performance failure of new such appointments only led to their eventual departure and move on to seek more lucrative employment elsewhere.

After Simon Susman moved on to the position of CEO, the first senior appointment was that of Andrew Jennings *(2007-2010)* who was head hunted from his position as head of SAKS, Fifth Avenue in New York.

He was an eccentric, single-minded character with very little knowledge of Woolworths and one of his first initiatives was to attempt to adapt Woolworths into a business model of a departmental store. Much effort was initially spent to introduce famous branded cosmetics to supplement the Woolworths branded products and relocate the position of the department at the entrance of the store similar to that seen in Greatermans, Garlicks and Stuttafords all of whom are relics of the past. Edgars is still hanging in there for dear life, but as this is being written, the media are reporting that they are on the brink of collapse putting 140 000 jobs at risk which would make it the biggest single job loss ever in South Africa and would deal a massive psychological blow to the South African economy.

The real challenge was however to negotiate with the leading cosmetic houses to allow Woolworths to stock the really well known brands but more often than not because of the long standing relationships with stores such as Edgars and Stuttafords who had exclusivity rights on the most popular products, Woolworths had to be satisfied with the lesser known brands.

His approach was the promotion of shop within shop concepts and soon the Australian Trenery brands and Country Road labels were evident in stores.

The other most vigorous drive was what he claimed to be his creation, was called the "nine box grid" which was really only in effect a product mix grid that resembled a modification of the retail base theory which is applied in some form or other by most retailers.

A well-received concept that was introduced was the American conception of "Town Hall" talks as a communication format at outside locations where business updates of each trading area was presented and kept the entire business well informed of the strategic intent and performance.

After his contract expired, it was not renewed.

Andrew Jennings was replaced by the then head of Country Road, Ian Moir (*2010-current*) who arrived with a credible reputation and a good track record and was known to have a harmonious relationship with Simon Susman. Even at the time it was speculated that he was earmarked to take over as CEO when Simon Susman retired.

Ian Moir brought stability and a sense of sensibility to the business which had up until then been lacking during the Andrew Jennings term but the focus was more on the strategic objectives of the business with the core principles of the business being spoken about but with lesser assessment and drive to ensure that they were delivered.

A whole host of other foreign appointees were made and to my mind eventually the entire entrenched culture and principles were all but decimated. Some appointees remained longer than others but in general their residence was relatively short.

To illustrate some examples of foreign and local appointees and their impact on the business, both positive and negative are listed below.

Carol Grollman came as part of the package with Farrel Ratner. Carol was at the time the head of marketing at Edgars who were very active in this space. Woolworths was on the other hand almost completely stagnant in the arena of effective marketing across all aspects. It was therefore no surprise that when she arrived it was no different to a whirlwind spiralling through the building as she brought an energy and strategy to establish a dynamic marketing department. Terry Brewis was the sole marketing representative in the foods group who single handily was driving promotions with a drive and passion. It was natural therefore that Carol took Terry under her wing and the journey began at a pace that I have never seen before. When one visited stores, it was blatantly apparent that there was no clear corporate identity as every store had different signage. The brands of product did not identify Woolworths on the labels but men's and boys products carried the Servus label while ladies and girls displayed the Princess label while baby wear carried a name of a daughter of one of the family. There was no advertising in any media apart from the seasonal sale which was compiled by the central merchandising area. So all in all, Carol had a blank sheet and the support of the directorate to transform the dull and dreary efforts that had been in existence for many years.

The first task she performed was to create an identity across all stores with an identifiable logo which was supported by uniform typeface across all products, packaging and communications which was strictly controlled by the marketing department to ensure that any deviation from the policy was not tolerated with the objective being that it looked that one person had created the designs, which in a sense was true as Carol set up a separate area under an executive to perform this task. Advertising programmes were structured and advertising agents were appointed to ensure a common professional thrust to all campaigns across both foods and clothing which included for the first time utilising television as a medium to target potential customers. The promotion calendar was set up and although some of the commercial departments took some time to embrace the concepts it soon became a way of life.

Some forms of measurement of the success of campaigns were introduced which although were quite rudiment in the beginning were at least an effort to motivate and justify the benefits of the initiatives. More accurate forms of customer profiling also brought a new dimension to developing mechanisms for the targeting of the correct customer. Without doubt it can be said that Carol set the foundations of what is today a sophisticated and very professional area of the business.

Around about the same time Norman Thompson was head hunted from a leading local courier network where he was credited with the structure and logistical design. His contribution to Woolworths was to set up the end to end logistical arm including the warehousing operation which he did so efficiently that the same principles that he introduced are still strictly applied to this day. It was not surprising that he went on to become the financial director where he built a highly efficient organisation with stable management.

After Mark Canning moved on to be head of Clothing, there was a mediocre holding operation in Central Planning area until Jeff Summers was imported from the Foot Locker in the United Kingdom. While Jeff came with considerable experience and logical business sense he was unfortunately caught in the middle of a power struggle in the form of Andrew Jennings who was determined to make his mark together with Andrew Levermore, a consultant from the United Kingdom at the same time. At the time, the stock levels were at unacceptable levels and the two Andrews decided that in an effort to reduce the stocks quickly was to embark on a Black Friday campaign as was successfully applied in the United States. The imposition of significant deep cut discounts to all products without exception that included the faster selling short stocked merchandise for one day was planned. Jeff objected vigorously calling it "retail suicide" and thereby basically formulated his own marching orders. The reality was that when the Black Friday in November arrived, it brought on an absolute riot and stores were overwhelmed with eager customers enjoying the incredible bargains. The unfortunate part was that the current better selling products were completely sold out in no time with the slow selling goods being left behind and as a result the offer for high holiday season sales consisted mostly of the least wanted product. Before leaving Jeff told me that as the head of the Central Merchandising group that he was made to be the fall guy.

The vacancy was filled by a recruit from Tesco, United Kingdom. Paula Disberry did not appear to have extensive merchandising expertise and relied heavily on her direct reports, being the group merchandise heads to guide her before making decisions. It was clearly apparent that her main objective was the fulfilment of her own personal set down goals. While this is not a bad thing it was done at all costs. One of the major goals was the achievement of the set down BEE targets in terms of the staff mix of colour and gender. I suspect that there was also a personal preference of building the female component in particular. Consequently there was a systematic retrenchment and restructuring exercise whereby some unfortunate highly experienced and skilled males at very short notice were offered packages and departed the building taking invaluable knowledge with them. The replacements were invariably female and brought not much in the way of experience and talent to the table but eventually the achievement of the BEE targets were much improved benefiting Paula's personal goals. As is normal in most planning models, the planning function operates from company level and then cascades down to group and department level across all locations. In an effort to reduce operating costs of her area of control, Paula was keen to divorce the high company planning level and that of the groups which is almost like removing one's head and still expect the body to work independently. This had the consequence that disciplines were compromised and central guidance was forfeited resulting in a situation of out of control inventories.

Another major action which was close to my heart was the disbanding of the central support team which was under my control who were fondly known as "Charlies Angels" when the decision was taken. The centralised support team was very successful in both it's structure and roles. The group consisted of an proficient team of twelve who each were capably responsible for a function, an application or area. Their main responsibilities was the training and support of users, interaction with the IT development teams, system testing and the maintenance of central foundation data. The team acted as a central help desk or point of contact the logistics group, suppliers, departments and store operations. Based on the fact that this support structure seemed to be unique to Woolworths in comparison to global practices it was decided without apparent appreciation or understanding of the valuable contributions they made that the functions should be absorbed into the groups with accountability being handed over to the group planning heads most of whom were not adequately informed to perform this function.

This action was considered to be absurd by the users and other contact areas in the business but nevertheless it was implemented and all members of the support team were offered retrenchment packages or the option to seek alternative positions in the business. The irony was that almost all members opted for the packages and a goldmine of knowledge was on the brink of being lost.

Fatefully the IT group, who were the most affected by this seemingly senseless decision, apart from the fact it reduced the operating costs, created almost a replica group of support and quite a few of the original team members simply moved to the IT group either on a permanent or contract basis. Nevertheless the quality of comprehension and performance benchmarks in the groups deteriorated substantially in a very short period of time.

The introduction of foreign appointees was not limited to the mainstream areas but also touched other areas such as Foods and Logistics. In the Logistics area Phil Davies who was credited with the design of the logistical systems of the GAP chain of stores joined initially as a highly paid consultant. Without doubt he was determined to make his impact and set about redesigning the supply chain from end to end with an air of ruthlessness. This resulted in a deep rift of relationships within the Supply Chain area as well as in some areas in the Central Merchandising group. He nevertheless persisted and in the changeover of the removal of the support area I was assigned to be part of his system design efforts and supplier and warehouse performance management. Apart from being rigid in his ways he was often impulsive and frequently guilty of unpredictable explosive behaviour which made working with him quite stressful. During this time Burger van der Merwe, a born and bred Woolworths person to the core, who was the head of the logistics area and for who I had immense respect was also an unfortunate casualty of a restructuring exercise together with much political dogfighting and was subsequently removed from his station. Sadly as he was not prepared to accept alternative positions offered to him and he was lost to one of the major competitors. (Fortunately he has subsequently returned to Woolworths as head of store operations) Eventually the replacements were not sustained until the number two ran the area, Willem Immelman, who had a vehement divergent rapport with Phil Davies. As a result, a consistent ongoing encounter between the two continued. As Phil had the ear of Paula Disberry, it was no surprise when Phil was appointed as head of the supply chain area and he was quick to remove those together with Willem Immelman who he considered to be obstacles or unqualified and implemented a significant people reorganization in the area. Phil embarked on some radical modifications to the supply chain and warehousing systems. He too has subsequently left the business, but this was after I had left so, I cannot comment on the reasons why or the state of his area of control.

In summary, after siting the more significant examples of the influence of the influx of so called retail wizards above, on balance it is my assessment that the organisation suffered not only in the financial arena but also the cultural philosophies were severely damaged more than any benefits derived from the pursuance of this strategy.

FRANCHISE STORES – THE DOWNFALL

In the mid-eighties Woolworths embarked on a programme of franchising of stores in mostly smaller or out of the way towns commencing with Gaberone in 1988 which initially was both a foods and clothing store. From there some satellite stores were established and the owner Isch Handa became a formidable entrepreneur in the expansion of the franchise models which in 2010 consisted of seventy-six stores owned by thirty-seven franchisees. Most of the owners had previous experience of

Woolworths and therefore maintained the principles and culture in their own investments. Most stores were very successful which can be mainly attributed to the passion and trading abilities of the owners who had intimate knowledge of their customers.

The purchase of stocks took the form of a buying week for each season held at head office whereby the forthcoming season's ranges were presented, and the stores simply ordered the quantities and product mix which best suited their stores. Very often this was done with specific customers in mind and the unique profile of their market.

In 2010 however, Woolworths announced to their South African franchisees that it would be ceasing the local franchise businesses and that they would buy all local franchises at a fair value. The reasons given were that after a strategic review they had come to the conclusion that it was no longer in their best interests to continue operations as it did not wish to be both a franchiser and an operator as it had become increasingly more complex and expensive to operate a separate franchise business model with its own systems and processes.

A commitment was made that the stores would be bought as going concerns and that all staff would still be offered employment. If any stores were not prepared to enter into the agreement, they would be able to continue with lesser support until their contracts expired and then would simply be taken over. Very few, if any opted for this option.

It was speculated that Woolworths might have come to the conclusion that the cost associated with the franchise model, outweighed the benefits and that it would much rather keep all of the margin for itself. However, if this was valid it was probably true due to the concentrated focus that was applied by the owners themselves. Through absorbing the stores into the corporate structure that the focus would be lost as the turnovers were relatively small compared to the larger units which were set as the priority very much according to the eighty twenty principle where the top twenty percent of stores contributed eighty percent of the turnover. Previously the stores were offered the full range whereas under the corporate stable the product mix was limited to much smaller catalogues and received very little specialized attention. The performance of the individual stores consequently deteriorated significantly.

While the international stores continued, it was with great difficulty, primarily because the partners that were selected did not adhere to or share the principles of the brand. Governmental restrictions, cultural, logistical and infrastructural complications in Africa made it incredibly difficult to conduct business and consequently stores such as Nigeria were closed. With the purchase announcement for local franchises it was noted that it also ended of franchise stores in African countries in the future. Woolworths owned 33 stores through franchise agreements in Botswana, Namibia, Swaziland and Ghana, which contributed a combined annual turnover of R1.1 billion. Some of these stores became part of a joint venture with the franchisee, Isch Handa who was appointed as a non-executive director of Woolworths in Botswana and Namibia.

Within head office effectively the franchise group was disbanded with the retrenchment of executive and senior management positions all of whom were extremely talented and under very difficult conditions achieved a huge amount of success while other staff were redeployed.

SYSTEMS DEVELOPMENT

Woolworths was a very late starter in the automation of its business. After the decision to go ahead with the computerisation, one of the first projects that was initiated was that of ECL in the mid-eighties, a project headed up by Tom Stephens which entailed the electronic conversion of the laborious function of manual completion of the checking list by people with carbon paper and sturdy pens and the use of courier services to get the documents to head office. The electronic version allowed the data to captured on a computer and then transmitted electronically to the Wooltru computer services where electronic print outs were generated and delivered to the respective departments. At this point a fully-fledged IT department was evolving under the guidance of Christo Barnard and the programmers, project managers and user groups became a new being in the life of Woolworths as from the late eighties and beginning nineties. The initial focus was the generation of replica manual functions such as the sales and stock reports, the placement of electronic orders and some basic analytical tools. A fundamental error that was made is that it was decided to utilise the same programming platform as that used at M&S with some modifications to suit Woolworths needs. This application was known as Model 204 but quite soon thereafter the shortcoming that there was no technical support available in South Africa to maintain or enhance the programmes caused some cumbersome and uncomfortable situations when things went wrong both in the Foods and Clothing environments. In addition to the mainframe Model 204 application some stand-alone UNIX systems were independently developed and the fact that there was no integration between the two platforms led to considerable mistrust in the integrity of the data and so often it was an easy cop out to blame "the system".

The custodianship of system resided in central areas in both foods and clothing although there were naturally very different applications. I was fortunate enough to have exposure to both sides as being part of the centralized teams. In the Foods group much focus was placed on the development of systems that delivered orders dependent on availability of perishable product using algorithms that took into account sales, shelf life and delivery patterns with the objective of maximising sales with the minimisation of waste. What I found quite interesting that at the time the Foodies were often referred to as the cowboys of the business and as such possessed merchanting skills which were mainly nothing other than "gut feel." Therefore, it was a major challenge to attain the acceptance of computerised conclusions and too often these were overwritten with a stroke of the pen. It took a while to correct this behaviour.

In later years the concept of space planning on store shelves became another significant factor in the merchandising of the food markets. This resulted in a constant battle to sell products as much as possible with none of it passing the expiry date while at the same time keeping the shelves full all the time.

The centralised support team in Foods for the sake of a name was known as the Distribution Group that provided support in the form of coaching to the buying groups, the administration of loading and removal of the products from the system and were involved in the placement of orders and determination of regional availability with suppliers.

On the clothing side, the integrated role fell under the umbrella of a Central Planning group. The primary function of this group was also the maintenance of static data but added to that it had to control the total intake required down to merchandise group level in order that the total company sales, stock and write down targets were met. This function, which through weekly meetings with group merchandise heads, was pedantically performed by Peter Bazlington who, because of his fanatical attention to detail often did not make him the most popular kid on the block but nevertheless earned him immense respect. I firmly believe the frequently quoted comment in the annual reports during the eighties and nineties that "once again stocks were tightly controlled" can be attributed to the hawk eye of Peter Bazlington. Simon Susman often said that if "Peter says it is right than it is right!"

Even in the eighties Woolworths lacked a complete merchandise planning system such as that which Truworths and Foschini enjoyed in the form of a product called Arthur. The process of departmental planning was very disjointed and lacked a consistent approach. In order to rectify this Guy Wilson was appointed by Syd Muller in the early nineties to head up Central Planning and put some disciplined structure into the business planning function.

I had the privilege to work under Guy Wilson and considered him as a mentor and without doubt a retail genius albeit that he was a bit quirky in his manner. Guy was head hunted from the Foschini group where he was the Managing Director of their Pages chain of stores at the time. On the side line together with a partner he founded a small chain of stores known as Sheet Street for which he developed all the systems almost as a hobby. Quite a bit later he once showed me his original scribbled format of the planning system that was the birth of planning systems like that of Arthur used by Foschini and was the forerunner of that which was being developed for Woolworths.

At the time two independent contractors, Richard von Hirschberg and John Manning were appointed with a small team of programmers to build the Woolworths specified planning system which they named Mokoro, after a traditional dugout canoe-like vessel commonly used in the Okavango Delta as a popular mode of transport. The advantage of outsourcing the task had obvious potential financial benefits for them and they had the Woolworths infra structure to utilise and stress test. The agreement was that the product would be exclusive to Woolworths in South Africa and they were able to market it overseas. As a user and part of the sign off group it was not uncommon that I would find myself providing on their behalf my views of my hands-on experience to potential overseas customers. Towards the end of the project during a meeting, Richard von Hirschberg received a phone call from IBM informing him that they had decided to purchase the system. The rest is history with Richard living on a horse ranch in America and one of the programmers spends most of his time on the beach in Plettenberg Bay.

Life with Guy Wilson continued to be extremely stressful not only for him but also those of us who had to work under him. This was due to the fact shortly after Syd Muller appointed Guy who was to report directly to him, Farrel Ratner was hired as Managing Director and Guy was then expected to report to him. This was not acceptable to Guy and as a result communication ceased completely between the two. Peter Bazlington and I became the messengers between the two offices and as such had to endure the tensions and subsequent abuse from both sides. Eventually the situation became completely unsustainable to the extent that Colin Hall, the chairman of Wooltru at the time became involved and it ended with Guy being transferred to Truworths where he went on to become the Merchandise Director. He left Truworths after Mr Price made a bid for Sheet Street which he could not refuse.

At the same time, almost in tandem there was a project team developing an automated replenishment system, the concept of which was designed by Henk Conradie literally of the back of a cigarette box in the Diaz Tavern, a pub up the road from Woolworths. To this end a project team was put in place and run by Bertha Solsky to test the principles and it soon gained momentum and a full-on structural reshuffle took place.

My personal view of this initiative was that it is probably one of the greatest disasters which was so mismanaged and costly that it is surprising that Woolworths survived it. The theory was good and very exciting in that it was sold on the basis that for core, continuity products such as vests, underwear, white shirts, fleece tops, beige chino trousers and the like was when a store sold one, they automatically received one and the advantages was the consequent lower stock holdings that would be derived.

Under the Group Head leadership of Clive Richards an entire duplicate group for each department with location planners and managers and statistical analysts was set up as a centralised group which in itself was extremely costly.

The focus only on continuity lines divorced the control of them from the parent departments although the top line performance indicators for the department remained the responsibility of the parent department planner which was an impossible and unreasonable expectation.

A condition was imposed was there would be no interference or influence of the results that the replenishment system from the parent department. As a result, while the parent planner would set the budget as part of the departmental plan but if the replenishment planner felt it was too conservative the actual projection differed considerably and inevitably inflated the actual purchases from suppliers.

From the parent department perspective, the perception from group head down evolved that the replenishment lines could be planned conservatively as they would create their own projections and growth and be replenished accordingly. This would therefore free up budgets for non-replenishment exciting product which led to additional styles and colours that can only be defined as blatant irresponsible over buying.

Projections were given to suppliers at the beginning of each season and more often than not they would in the interests of economies of scale make the entire projection all in one go. Attempts were made to try and limit this practice but with limited success.

Stores were expected to have a full range of sizes and colours at all times and subsequently in the smaller stores automatically increased the stock quantities out of proportion to the sales.

The consequence of all of the above led to not only additional costs but put pressure on local suppliers to hold and finance higher stocks which led to Woolworths warehousing the product to relieve the burden on suppliers.

After the departure of Guy Wilson to Truworths, his position was filled by Mark Canning. A significant contrast was that he maintained a close relationship with Farrel Ratner, so it was no surprise when he was appointed, it was with expanded responsibilities. A notable change was the eradication of the manual Checking List that had been in the company since the beginning of the association with M&S and was captured by data capturers was replaced by the electronic checking list which was transmitted from stores into the merchandising system automatically. This was an example of a really successful project that was flawlessly implemented.

The other significant system development under the watch of Mark Canning was that of a data management system with the original Anderson consulting team initiating the guidelines. After a global controversy involving Anderson Consulting the team became known as Reagola and worked tirelessly developing the Retek system to meet the requirements of Woolworths and one could say considering the enormity of the task, the creation of the product was virtually faultless.

In order to put it in context, a master data management system provides a repository of product information that enables efficient synchronisation among internal retail applications and external stakeholders such as suppliers, warehouses and logistics.

The most common processes comprehended in the master data management solutions are typically source identification, data collection, data transformation, rule administration, error detection and correction, data consolidation and the distribution of data throughout the organisation to ensure consistency and control in the ongoing maintenance and application of this information.

Mark Canning went on to be head of clothing where he remained until his untimely departure.

I had the benefit of heading up the user group support team that was responsible for the support, testing, training and implementation amongst the users under the Woolworths sponsorship team that was unfortunately led by mediocre, misinformed, and egotistical management which regrettably created tense relationships between the user groups, Supply Chain group, IT specialists and the project team in the efforts to bring about a smooth successful implementation of the venture.

In spite of the numerous challenges and disruptions created by a series of inept management and leadership during the earlier to mid 2000 -2010 years the eventual successful introduction of the Retek data management systems brought Woolworths up to date and on par with system dependencies which were evident in the rest of the retail industry.

THE WOOLWORTHS CARD
In 1994, Woolworths introduced its store card. Woolworths Financial Services, a joint venture between Woolworths South Africa and Barclays Bank, was incorporated in 2000 to provide Woolworths customers with focused financial products and services. In 1994 the reaction to the launch of the card was absolutely explosive, so much so that the stock levels fell so dramatically that in certain stores the stocks virtually ran out. This was particularly evident in those stores where the lay bye systems where customers purchased products and they were stored, and instalments were made until the full amount was paid off and the goods could then be collected. A typical store was Mitchells Plain where the uptake of the card was as high as sixty percent and when the goods were bought the customer could take immediate possession. Stock levels in such a store could be normally targeted at seven to eight weeks after the launch. Of the card the stock levels dropped to an equivalent of two weeks' worth of forward sales. The success of the card was such that it was nothing short of a riot and sales turnover escalated phenomenally and thus Woolworths entered the credit market and the concept was furiously followed by many other retailers.

The Woolworths Store card can be used at any store to pay water and electricity utility bills, purchase airtime, automatically be part of all WRewards programme to enjoy an additional 5% off promotions and link to the My School, My Planet, My Village fund raising initiatives.

Other products that are on offer by Woolworths Financial services are the Woolworths in-store card; gold credit card; black credit card and revolving personal loans.

THE CHANGE FROM MERCHANDISE LED TO BUYING LED BUSINESS
Up until the latter part of the nineties the business was driven be the merchandising arm whose basic tasks were to guide the buying arm to buy goods within the parameters of the budgets. Whether the product was basic core , high fashion or car tyres ,the principles remained the same. The intake plans were created by the merchandising arm and the buying arm identified the new seasons trends both in colour and style utilising the historical performance and purchased in accordance to the plans. If it so happened that a buyer wished to become a merchandise manager it was a prerequisite that they first qualify as a merchandiser and gain a clear understanding of the business acumen end of the role prior to being considered for promotion to a merchandise manager heading up a team of buyers and merchandisers and the support assistants for both these roles. Bret Kaplan was heading up clothing at the time and was passionate about merchandise and trends and

was fully committed to the fact that the business should be driven by the buying arm and be supported by the merchandise role.

After motivating this concept it was accepted in principle by the directorate which initiated the reorganisation of the clothing buying departments.

Firstly, a design group was created whose members have a deep insight into the market they are targeting through the analysis of the changing trends and use these to provide creative direction and develop product designs for the buying teams to consider.

Usually these participants tend to think out of the box and their creative minds can challenge some of the comfort zones of other team members. What must be kept top of mind is that they need to consistently apply their intellect way ahead of time as to what they think the customer requires as opposed to their personal desires.

Typically, the character traits which they will possess are that they are independent, spontaneous, extroverts, driven by ideas and are confident by nature. Their real challenge was to convince the buying teams and senior management to buy into their vision and have the confidence that what they have in mind will be commercially acceptable to the customer

The buyer on the other hand needs to have a clear understanding of the product that is required which is in line with the trend guidelines best suited to their target customer profiles for both the high fashion segment as well as those that best serve the more traditional customer.

It is a fact is that the role of the designer and the buyer may be a bit blurred in that they research the same fashion forecasting sites and other sources of inspiration in order to put a range of garments together. Both roles must be aware of sizing, quality and costs related to fabrics, trimmings and production. To achieve this successfully they must be flexible enough to develop and buy the most suitable product that is in line with the prescribed strategy and achieves the desired profit margin in keeping with the set down targets. The evaluation of competitive activity and product ranges through regular store visits and comparative shopping provides the knowledge required to keep ahead of the field.

The buyer has to be multi-talented in that as well as being creative they also need to monitor the sales objectively and be flexible enough to react accordingly in terms of turning on or turning off production and transferring fabric and components to more appealing product styles where sales performance and fast emerging trends dictate.

What is key to be a successful buyer is the ability to work as part of the overall team and influence the rest of the team's activities which could be in the form of a managerial and developmental capacity that could also include both their peers and superiors.

The merchandisers work can best be described by a novelty t-shirt on the market which has the following statement blazon across the front panel which reads as follows – *"Merchandise Planner – we do precision guesswork based on unreliable data by those of questionable knowledge"*. Although the humour can be appreciated it should be known that this statement is not too far from the truth as the success of merchandising objectives is reliant on many diverse inputs.

The merchandiser or planner applies their focus on maximising profitability from the business end. This is done largely through the analysis of historical sales and the influence of the trend direction to determine the range categories and product breakdown within the overall sales budget.

The merchandiser's job has to be to provide guidance to the buyer to procure within the budget parameters. In short it can be described as providing the buyer with a shopping list or range plan that allows them to go out and fill in the blanks on the plan while buying product. This activity requires the careful management of the "open to buy" which can often be a source of tension between the buyer who always tends to want more and the merchandiser who holds the purse strings. A good deal of emotional maturity and teamwork on both sides is therefore critical for a successful partnership.

As though with a wave of a wand departmental heads were now those with a buying background but magically instantly became planning experts overnight. It was only natural that the planning fraternity felt that this was a setback, and thus led to all sorts of complications. The descriptions outlined above clearly illustrates the vastly different traits required by the roles and there is a distinct division of left and right thinking. In my particular situation I suddenly found that my buyer who had absolute zero planning knowledge and nor was he interested to have any as he was a wonderful creator but did not have any analytical competencies and basic business acumen whatsoever. One of the most profound questions I have had to answer in my career during a follow up meeting on one occasion with him was "how do I know you are not lying to me?" Another experience I had, was where a buyer who was now expected be proficient in the planning role and was due to have a performance assessment meeting with her planner came to me and asked, "what questions should I ask Mr. X?" While this appears to be mildly amusing it unfortunately brought with it some serious implications. The planning function was expected to guide the buyers to buy within the parameters of the budget using sophisticated planning tools.

In reality some of the newly elevated buyers had no respect for the merchandisers and overrode the merchandisers who in their opinion were just "computer jockeys" and simply over bought not only in quantities, but also in numbers of ways of styles and colours which had devastating consequences in terms of the proliferation of ranges. When the time came for performance assessments and the merchandiser was challenged as to why their key performance indicators were not met and the merchandiser explained that the actions were on the buying manager's instruction, the response was that they should have been more assertive in effectively influencing the buy. In one particular occurrence, the merchandiser lost her job as a result.

Other drawbacks were the fact that the product mix was distorted by the buying wishes rather than what the customer wants were. As a result, the choices were not driven by the budget and that type of product that was considered too "trad" (traditional) were dropped in favour of more adventurous merchandise. Classic examples were in the men's shirt department where the thirty million rand a year basic polyester/cotton easy care shirt ideal for work wear over a wide variety of colours was virtually eradicated and replaced by pure cotton shirts which, while being beautiful were hard to iron and came at a higher price. A similar example was the fast selling linen blend shirt which was neat and easy care was replaced by pure linen which was offered hanging out of its pristine packaging. They were rejected entirely by the traditional customer and hung on the rack looking like washing on the washing line.

The popular farmer type shirts that were hard wearing with coloured patch pockets were discontinued but the rural franchise stores continued to buy these independently in significant volumes.

The Pilot shirt with epaulettes, flap dual pockets and a slit for the pen which Woolworths had captured the entire market for airline pilots, security firms and other uniforms were discontinued at the intense displeasure of the customers.

In the children's departments the entire range of party dresses which sold in massive volumes especially for events such as Eid were removed from display. All of these products were handed on a platter to very appreciative competitors.

After a while it became clearly evident that this organisational structure was not a great option and the groups were adapted whereby they were led by a buying head and a planning head. The structure was an improvement but nevertheless there were still conflict situations which were more often than not won by whoever had the most dominant personality.

THE CHANGE OF SUPPLER BASE PHILOSOPHIES

Just prior to the latter part of the period 2005 to 2010 the trend of sourcing product out of the east emerged at a rapid pace with the major benefits being that of cost saving, especially if the company had access to quota relief from tariff duties which Woolworths did have of their own as well as that of a supplier who had abundant relief and was willing to release this to Woolworths and goods were bought through this vehicle for a fee so healthy product margins were achieved for a period of three or four years. Darren Todd, who was a sourcing specialist in the United Kingdom returned to South Africa to head up the technology and more importantly the sourcing departments.

The researching of new, cheaper, innovative and exciting sources of supply in order to maintain a competitive advantage in the market place is an ongoing process, as is the need to maintain a sustainable relationship with current core suppliers which comes with a continual effort to improve their delivery standards of product. Suppliers are expected to be consistently reliable, effective and efficient to retain the business of their clients as the success of the retailers is the guarantee of continued acceptance of the product that they produce.

A constant balance of those products which are sourced from local suppliers and that which are manufactured off shore is important. As off shore suppliers improved in terms of quality, equipment and workforce living standards there was an increasing pressure on costs and therefore the sources did not remain geographically static.

Fashion buying was originally focused in the Far East in Hong Kong and Taiwan, but costs were increasing faster than they had in the past as well as pressure was being placed on authorities to elevate minimum wage bands. It is therefore not surprising that production was moved to more cost-efficient areas such as Indonesia, Bangladesh, Pakistan, Cambodia, and Vietnam while production in Madagascar and Mauritius also became prevalent.

Hong Kong and Taiwan have now become more the management and design centres who procure from alternative production plants. The ease of increased technology, the relaxing of bureaucratic barriers as well as cheaper travel enabled the transfer of production to be relatively easy and flexible.

Migration of production to newer countries brought limitations and therefore it was important to maximise efficiencies in the current countries where goods were produced while at the same time sourcing alternative manufacturing plants that would meet the ethical and quality standards.

Added to this is the probability that the larger the offshore supplier is, the more the likelihood is that the retailer will be less important in their lives and if need be, the order can be more easily forfeited. A real example is that of men's basic polyester cotton shirts which primarily was the bulk of the local factory's capacity and the sales turnover from this particular line was in the region of thirty million rand per year. When an offer of the high volumes from China at very much cheaper cost prices, the production was quickly shifted off shore. Unfortunately, after Cambridge shirts shut down their plants producing this line, the China source came back and informed Woolworths that they had a more lucrative offer to fill their capacity and therefore would not meet their commitment. The converse is that if the overseas supplier is small, the possibility exists that the production may be outsourced to other vendors who the retailer may not even know about.

Overseas factories seldom readily have excess production capacity and that this together with the longer transport lead times make the possibility of repeat orders within the same season improbable.

Sourcing internationally does, at face value, often appears to be very attractive but there are factors that need to be taken into account which can lead to additional unforeseen costs as well as logistical. challenges particularly in terms of lead times. The re-organisation of production can therefore be perplexing and the savings that may be apparent up front could indeed be decimated later down the line for which Woolworths have countless examples.

Keeping track of the off-shore supply chain at times presents some complex challenges and makes it very difficult to monitor the progress of product at all times. An extreme illustration of such a scenario is where the process commences with the raw material producer who passes the product onto the commodities traders whose purchasing agents sells them onto the garment manufacturers. In the procedure local distributors could be involved to deliver the raw materials to the garment manufacturing plant. Secondary vendors for outsourced processes are frequently utilised before the product is delivered eventually to the local exporters and freighters administered by agents on behalf of the larger trading houses who are the frontline liaison with the retailer.

Advantages may be enjoyed by having a dedicated foreign office in key cities to control the management of suppliers and product. Woolworths opened up their China office in Shanghai. Obviously, this does come at an added cost and should only be considered when a critical mass in that foreign country is achieved. However, the formation of such an organisation must be assessed on merit as to whether it is viable or not. Typically, such a team will consist of two or three merchandisers, possibly buying and sourcing specialists together with maybe three or four quality controllers who spend two to three days a week in the factories focusing exclusively on the retailer's orders. The foreign office owns the relationship with the supplier and are able to exert pressure to ensure critical deadlines are met. Communication is easier and faster as such teams are self-managed and can be flexible in evaluating priorities.

The extreme example of the complexity of dealing with offshore suppliers is that of the world's largest trading house being the Hong Kong based sourcing and logistical company, Li Fung. They own no factories or mills but simply play matchmaker between poor countries factories and vendors which have favourable labour rates and costs and the global retailers for whom Li Fung handle the logistics.

Li Fung represent some fifteen thousand suppliers across sixty countries which enable them to procure very high volumes and have them produced in a fraction of a time that a single supplier would take to complete. It is not surprising that consequently they are known as the "Walmart of purchasing" and the thousands of tons of production makes it difficult to pin point the true sources of the product and they have been alleged from time to time to be linked to several calamities in some dubious factories across a range of locations mainly China, Bangladesh, Vietnam and many others.

I had the experience of setting up a supplier relationship whereby the design and head office was situated in Hong Kong, the production planning and orders were sent to an office in Shang Hai, the production took place in Vietnam and the goods were despatched from Shanghai, all of this was in order to achieve tariff savings and the benefit of cheaper labour costs.

Where the retailer is dominant in their target market and the volumes are substantial enough it is advantageous for them to cut out the middleman agent and procure directly from the source. By doing this an advantage is gained over their competitors and they do not end up subsidising the supply chain for their rivals especially where full containers are bought on a repeat basis. Advantage is also to be gained through using a buying agent or consolidator to combine the products into full container loads where they purchase from multiple off shore suppliers.

Currency exchange rate fluctuations may well change the advantage of buying off shore, as will quota limitations which could change in the exporting country due to the fact that costs will probably increase should the availability of the quotas become scarcer.

The management of offshore deliveries is more complex and if minimum order quantities are imposed, they can lead to higher storage costs and inventory investment together with varying transport charges all of which Woolworths experienced at various times.

The impact of the Chinese New Year is more profound than ever imagined. The planning for deliveries is complicated as it is a moving target every year but what is even more unpredictable is the uncertainty of the return of workers after the holidays. The reason for this is the fact that many manufacturing plants are situated closer to the ports while the workers return inland to their villages. When the time comes to return, many decide to stay away longer or not return at all.

The intricate nature of international freight forwarding requires either an in house dedicated team or the need to outsource this function to an agency to take on the responsibility which is what Woolworths chose to do. The downside is that there is a dependency on the agents reporting infrastructure to keep track of the progress of off shore deliveries.

Often the additional travelling and increased management costs are not taken into account when considering product quotations. The opening of foreign offices with sourcing, quality control and buying teams in itself can be a considerable additional overhead that needs to be established, staffed and equipped and is excluded from the base garment cost.

Frequently the bulk offshore deliveries have to be unpacked, repacked and labelled after allocation that results in multiple handling which adds considerable cost and time delay.

For the reasons above, the viability of sourcing from foreign suppliers has to be carefully considered in terms of the minimum volumes that need to be procured to achieve the benefits while at the same time being able to exceed the sales potential without putting strain on the warehouse storage capabilities which Woolworths began to find out more and more and therefore the process of returning back to local supply became increasingly attractive.

Alas, the damage had already been done and when one reflects on the number of formidable local suppliers that no longer exist and the fact that a real reluctance to re-invest in new plants is very distressing. Coupled to this was the number of jobs that were lost with the swing from generations of sewing skills, particularly in the Western Cape, to other industries is for me the saddest consequence.

In order to illustrate the extent of what losses were endured, one cannot but feel devastated when reflection on the past is conducted.

In the knitwear industry, Tej in Cape Town with a capacity of two million garments per year closed down in 2003. Verona in Cape Town producing 150,000 pieces per annum shut down in 2009. Other casualties were Peninsula Knitting Mills who shut down in the mid-nineties, Adonis in Johannesburg closed in 2007 while Baisch Knitwear in Cape Town ceased operation in 2012, Durban Knitting Mills ceased in the mid-eighties and Danco Knitting Mills, Cape Town closed during the mid-nineties.

In the tailoring and cut and sew sector there was an exodus of superb suppliers such as Rex Trueform, Bertish, Pals Clothing, Heriswell, Fairweather Fashions, Reviera Fashions, Bibette, Mathews and Swering, Manhattan in Salt River closed in 1999, and as recent as 2017 Peter Blond who were virtually exclusive suppliers to Woolworths terminated their operations.

Household shirt names that no longer exist are Peerless, Polo and Cambridge while even the dominant tie and handkerchief factories Skipper, Cravateur and Winkler are relics of the past.

A whole group of yarn spinners such as USM in Port Elizabeth closed in 2003, Tramatex in East London shut in 2009, Table Bay which had huge capacities and Knit spinners left the industry in 2008, Patons and Baldwins, SA Fine worsteds, SBH and Frame amongst others also disappeared.

It must be said that some of these premature closures was also due to the weakening rand in relation to the dollar which inflated the cost of raw material.

In recent years the substantial shift to high-volume cost-effective garment off shore manufacturers, the majority of which are based in the East has enforced domestically established suppliers and retailers in traditional manufacturing markets to review their modus operandi in order to keep their plants viable. As a result, more and more suppliers are placing emphasis on achieving the benefits of innovation, higher quality and speed in the production cycle where they may be manufacturing in lesser or varying volumes with shorter lead times. This enables them to be nimble enough to react to fashion swings rapidly particularly in an unpredictable market and thereby maintain a competitive advantage.

This objective is assisted by the choice of suitable production process configurations such as cellular groupings with the correct machinery and right attachments such as specialised folders. The needle and thread types should be such that they enable the efficient manufacture of the product type with lower inventory levels and lesser mark downs.

The advantage of quick response manufacturing is that it increases machine up time and therefore delivers an improved quality and subsequently less rework. Where this process is linked to a team incentive programme a consequence is lower staff turnover with fewer social noncompliance issues while also empowering employees and higher productivity.

Typical quick response initiatives are to have product stored at various stages of production so that it is possible to react swiftly to current consumer sales patterns. A prime example is where garments such as knitwear, sweaters, t-shirts, tank tops and the like are made up in uncoloured greige yarn and as the demand happens the garments are then piece dyed to whatever colours the market calls for. Not only in such cases is the benefit of improved sales achieved but it also reduces the build-up of unwanted garments or yarns. Other tactics include the reservation of production capacity but holding back the ordering of fabric and finalisation of the style for as long as possible in order to react more closely to trends as quickly as possible.

The logistics and supply chain functions need to be as streamlined as possible to allow the goods to reach the point of sale as quickly as possible which will require focus on storage, pick and pack operations, format in which the goods are best stored and transported, for example, whether they should be moved in a boxed or in a hanging state where the benefits of speed to market should be offset against the additional costs that will be incurred in setting up a hanging infra-structure.

With the explosion of sophisticated and faster computer systems, sales data is transferred in all sorts of variations and is thoroughly analysed in order to rapidly reveal the wants and preferences of consumers that enables quick collaborative decisions and forecast adjustments across the spectrum of mills, suppliers and retailers and through these actions Woolworths is able to better serve their customer in a faster time with less product proliferation which increases their competitiveness and offers the opportunity of potential growth of market share.

The sad fact is that with the frenzy to take advantage of the favourable deals that were offered by the East and the unfortunate impact that this had on the local industry as was illustrated by the demise of many institutions which were the back bone of the South African clothing sector resulted in a much weakened industry and the absence of specialized manufacturers, mills and other affiliated operations. Although the need has returned for local suppliers there are very few entrepreneurs that have the appetite to invest in the infrastructures which are required to accommodate the demand and the old age saying "once bitten twice shy" could never ring truer.

The challenge, therefore to convert the industry is extremely daunting in that there is no longer local supply of high capital cost plants of fabrics and yarns at local prices and therefore manufacturers are forced to import materials at exorbitant prices in order to protect a now non-existent industry if one considers that in the Western Cape alone once supported sixty thousand employees who by and large are no longer there.

QUALITY AND INNOVATION

Woolworths, like M&S were renowned for their attention to detail and the intrinsic specifications to which all fabrics and components and fabrics were sourced and selected. The sizing of all garments was all consistent that most often customers chose their clothing without having the need to try them on, so accurate was the consistency of the measurements.

For many years the technology and garment technology were guided by Harry Stein, a legend in his own right who then passed on the responsibility to David Glasser when he retired. Both gentlemen were acknowledged for their pedantic adherence to the set down standards. If production deviated from these standards, it was without hesitation that they were rejected in total whether they be still in the factory or in stores regardless as to the commercial deprivation to the company and the supplier. It was this philosophy that was so rigidly applied the built up the eternal abundant reputation and trust that customers placed in Woolworths and there are many examples where garments have been passed through familial generations through the endless durability and superb make up properties. The rigid testing processes which were tested in especially set up facilities included pilling experiments, wash tests, shrinkage, colour fastness, dye batch controls, scuff durability, sewing suitability, design matching and applications. Components such as buttons, applications and trimmings, labelling and the methods of attachment also endured the strict testing procedures. These were all according to a reference sample known as a black seal against which the first off production garment was signed off and was known as the red seal. Should any dispute materialize at a later stage in the bulk production, these seal garments were used as the point of reference to resolve any disputes.

Over the years Woolworths have kept their promise to earn the trust of their customers and set the benchmark for quality. Woolworths commitment to superior quality and value means they are always thinking of new ways to do things better and add more value to the customer's life.

While this intent is sincere it is not uncommon for exceptions to be evolve, in particular in the case of offshore procurements. Often control is lost in terms of exactly where goods are manufactured as the contracted manufacturer frequently outsources production and component procurement to "unknown" vendors. In spite of this, since 2013 substantial efforts have been made, of which I was very much part of, to identify rogue vendors and subject them to audits and ratings to limit such incidents.

Unfortunately, it is still really difficult at times to control in spite of quality controller inspections from the Woolworths office in Shanghai. A classic example is that Woolworths may approve garment label manufacturers at strategic locations close to the suppliers and insist that labels from these sanctioned suppliers only can to be used. The principle producer will for cost and time saving may prefer to use his cousin up the road to produce the labels very cheaply and have them at hand almost immediately.

Woolworths 'Farming for the Future' initiative is all about improving soil and water quality, saving water and encouraging biodiversity – without adding to the price. As part of their Good business journey, they're working with our farms to give back to nature and preserve our precious resources for generations to come.

Because Woolworths believes in the principles of responsible citizenship, they're focused on environmental and economic sustainability and building successful partnerships with their suppliers and communities to make sure our community is healthy, safe and secure. They are actively engaged in economic upliftment projects around South Africa and work with numerous small (often community-based) enterprises who supply them with everything from fresh herbs to beautiful bed and table linen.

Some of the initiatives that Woolworths have embarked on in their endeavors to make a difference in the sustainment of a healthy environment are:

- Woolworths are the first South African retailer to sponsor the Organic Exchange to drive South Africa's first commercial organic cotton crop.
- Woolworths send over 700 tons of plastic clothes hangers for recycling each year.
- Almost a third of the in-store signage is made of recycled materials and new stores use new shelving made from 90% recycled paper and 10% begasse from sugar cane.
- Woolworths donates over R250m of surplus food and clothing to needy charities each year.
- Woolworths stores have energy efficient light fixtures and automated lighting systems to cut their electricity consumption and carbon footprint.
- They're the only retailer that's part of the Worldwide Fund for Nature (WWF) Water Neutral Scheme, which means the water is balanced with projects to supply fresh, clean water into the environment.
- Trialling is done with two new, environmentally refrigeration technologies – one in the stores and another in some of the trucks that deliver food to the stores.
- Fresh foods are transported in plastic crates so there are no cardboard boxes to throw away, which has been the practice since 1967.
- Woolworths established the EWT Rhino Fund in conjunction with My Planet and the Endangered Wildlife Trust to help save our rhinos.

LOGISTICAL APPROACHES AND EFFECTS OF GLOBAL SOURCING

With the shift in the different types of procurement, Woolworths found itself in very different approaches required in the way that they had to accommodate the variance of storage and movement of stock which had to be catered for to best service the stores and ultimately the customer. To best describe this the various options are described below and the challenges and advantages that are presented.

CROSS DOCK OR FLOW THROUGH MODEL

This is the arrangement where the goods are pre-picked and packed at the mostly local supplier and are delivered to the distribution centre with store labels already gummed on the boxes or hanging sets. The alternative model of cross dock is where the order across the stores is delivered in bulk by the supplier to the cross-dock facility and the goods are picked by distribution centre staff and deposited directly in the respective store dispatch bays. Eventually the product from all suppliers for the day is consolidated in each store's designated bay awaiting transport.

Stores that are geographically far from the receiving distribution centre have the goods transhipped in bulk to their own respective closest geographical distribution centre where the picking operation will take place. The number and size of regional distribution centres are largely dependent on the density of the store network and the operating costs of such facilities. Woolworths main centres exist in Cape Town, Johannesburg and Durban.

The added benefit of the goods being picked and packed at the supplier is that the cartons are able to contain a combination of size and colour requirements by store and will therefore eliminate the need to unpack and repack from warehouse stock thus eliminating double handling and is subsequently more cost efficient. It is also possible where the supplier is picking multiple styles for the same store that these can be nested in the same container which reduces the need for additional packaging as well as reduces handling making for a considerable time saving.

In the event that there are over or short deliveries these cause delays as the changed quantity requires that the computer is updated, and the store quantities are scaled or recalculated based on varying algorithms that satisfy those stores with the greatest need first rather than simply apportioning equally across all the stores before the picking process can take place.

Where the receipt of product from suppliers are pre-labelled for stores, Woolworths conducts the testing of the accuracy by randomly inspecting a sample of cartons per supplier delivery and should the errors of packing fall outside of a certain tolerance it may result in the entire delivery being rejected. Instances where inaccuracies are within the tolerance but there is still a measure of incorrectness the error factor will still be extrapolated for the entire delivery and the invoicing is amended accordingly. Dependent on the size of the error it could attract a penalty. While many find this concept difficult for suppliers to accept, it should be remembered that the time and cost to do a full unpack and reconciliation in all likelihood would render the operation to be considered impracticable. Tests have been statistically done which reveal that the deviation from the sample survey results is also not that large.

The advantage of a flow through supply chain type is that the allocation can be made as late as possible allowing the shortening of the lead time and thereby meeting the customer demand more efficiently. The other benefit is also that the storage space requirement is minimal and dependent on the payment obligation it may be beneficial to the retailer in terms of cash flow in that ownership is only transferred upon receipt at the distribution centre.

There is an argument that utilising cross dock without warehousing is possibly a disadvantage in terms of the speed of delivery to stores as having stock drawn from the warehouse is quicker and smoother than waiting for the supplier delivery. The challenge is therefore to streamline the supplier delivery efficiencies to avoid the cost impact of holding warehoused stock and the handling costs that accompany this option which Woolworths does quite effectively for local suppliers.

·

Example of a cross dock flow through model

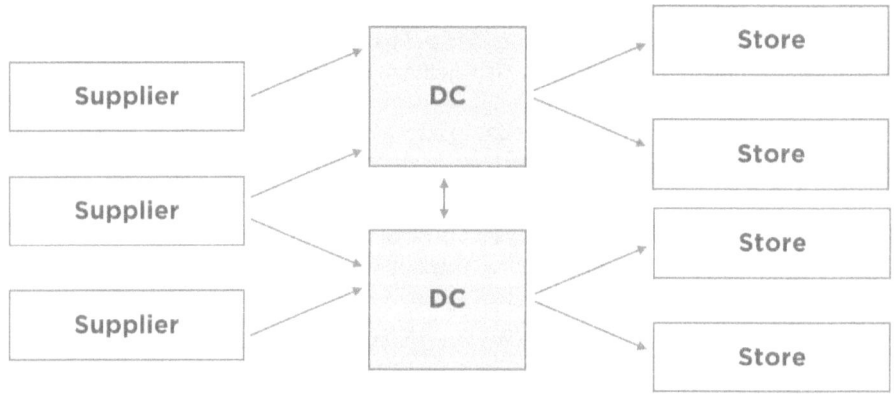

WAREHOUSED PRODUCT
is where the goods are received in bulk and are held in storage awaiting a call off and distribution to stores or to other storage sheds using the cross-dock facilities.

The warehouse can be seen to operate in a similar way as the supplier and performance management of indicators such as pick and pack accuracy, lead time measurement and the like can be implemented in the same way.

Warehoused stock tends to be predominantly for off shore product but may also include local suppliers particularly where minimum order quantities or negotiated special volume deals apply. In the main the products are continuity items with long supply lead times which are replenished on a regular basis as "pull" allocations.

The challenge with warehouse stock is to manage the stock levels as the investment in high volumes does not only have adverse financial consequences but also a real physical problem can arise in the form of space constraints and the possible requirement of additional operational resources. There are also instances of seasonal goods such as knitwear being produced in the off season to maintain a consistent production throughout the year and therefore creates an accumulation of stocks in the warehouse either at the supplier or the retailer at a cost which needs to be accounted for.

A point to note is that the storage shelving location is restricted to a fixed size which is usually the size of a pallet and may be at multi levels. As goods are withdrawn to the pick and pack locations it does happen that within one storage location a lesser quantity of goods remain behind which results in the space utilisation not being optimal as two different SKU's are not able to share the same location. Technically the warehouse becomes restricted in the capacity availability while physically this may not be the case. Thought needs to be applied to the minimum percentage or quantity that is able to be efficiently maintained and what tactics must be utilised regarding the consolidation of and removal of such stocks to free up the storage slots. This may take the form of allocating the odds to stores or transferring it to a different storage area with smaller slots and take on a high priority for distribution thereafter.

Other space inhibiting practices are where there are poor rates of sales, or volume deals are negotiated or through minimum order quantities that are imposed which cause the warehouses to fill up eventually and consequently result in the total utilisation of palette slots. The alternative then remains to either source outside storage, put the brakes on in terms of accepting intake or to simply stop buying to relieve the space and financial strain. The consequences of this is that availabilities suffer with the disruption of the composition of product and theme launches as well as the service levels of suppliers decline when they put production on hold while they wait for the retailer's stock levels to diminish and inevitably will sell on to other competitors in order to keep their production capacity full and operational.

The siting and the number of warehouses will be reliant on the geographic network of stores, the proximity to suppliers and ports and will be dependent on the achievement of the most economical costs which need to be continually reviewed to ensure the delicate balance of viability is maintained. I hold the belief that no matter how large the facility is, it will always be filled.

The introduction of higher levels of automation and the possibility of outsourcing operations to contractors or independent logistical organisations for storage and the management of the fleet of transport to tranship between storage points and schedule deliveries to stores also has an impact on the sustainability of economically viable facilities.

After the unloading of a container or truck at the back door, the cartons are consolidated and received, and then palletized for packing away in the storage facilities with unique identification location barcodes for ease of retrieval upon withdrawal in bulk.

After drawing product in bulk from the shelves the goods are moved to a pick and pack location to satisfy each store order and are deposited in the unique store bays to await dispatch.

The flow of product within a warehouse environment is illustrated below

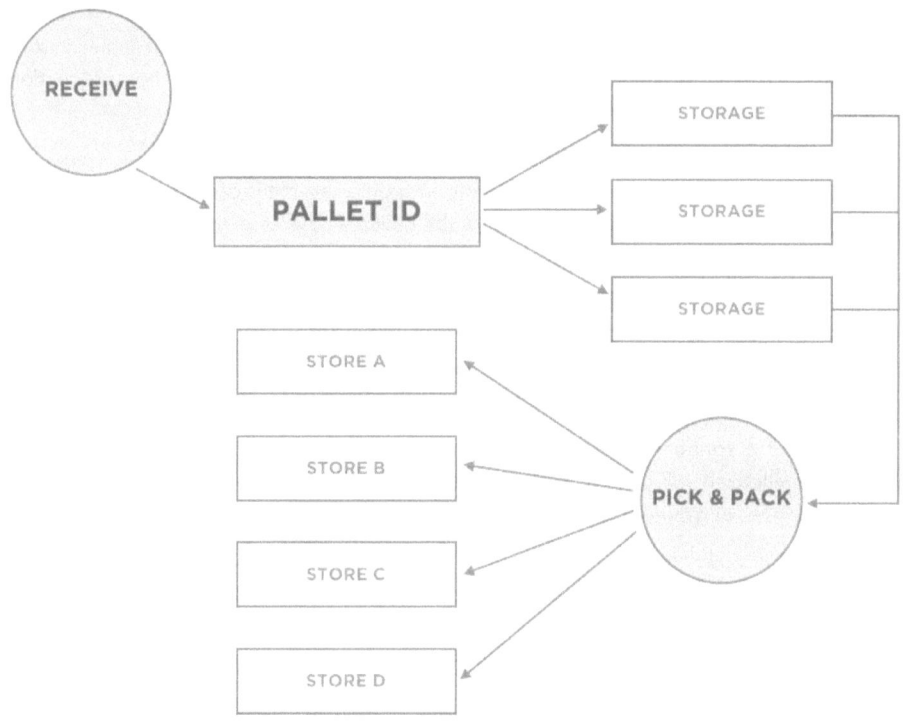

SHIFT TO PROCUREMENT OF NEW GLOBAL BUSINESSES

In 1997, WHL acquired a controlling interest in the Australian Country Road Group, with the remaining shares acquired in 2014. The Country Road brand was founded in 1974 as a manufacturer and supplier of women's casual cotton shirts. The brand was re-launched in 2004 and has evolved into a leading lifestyle brand renowned for stylish, high quality apparel, accessories, and homeware.
Country Road Group has subsequently expanded into a house of brands by the acquisitions and development of new strategies such as those listed below

- Launching Trenery in 2009 for customers who appreciate the beauty of simple, sophisticated collections that are modern in approach and classic in style;
- Acquiring Witchery, an Australian 'style authority' fashion brand, in 2012;
- Acquiring Mimco in 2012, offering accessible, luxury accessories with a quirk
- Acquiring Politix, a leading Australian menswear brand, in 2016.

On 1 August 2014, WHL acquired David Jones for a significant A$2.2bn. David Jones opened its first store in Sydney in 1838 with a mission to sell "the best and most exclusive goods." There are now more than 40 David Jones stores throughout Australia and New Zealand offering customers the best brands across fashion, beauty, and home. David Jones is not only Australia's oldest department store but is also the oldest department store in the world still trading under its original name.

With effect from 1 September 2017, a new regional Australian corporate and operational structure, Woolworths Australia, was introduced and operates out of its head office in Melbourne, Australia. The Woolworths South Africa division and WHL Group head office remained in Cape Town.

The Group now has more than 15 million customers, employs more than 46 000 employees across 14 countries, and trades in more than 1 500 store locations.

The acquisitions did not only place a substantial pressure on the financial aspects of the company, there was also a significant burden to put in place the most appropriate talents and management. In order to achieve this, it resulted in a drain of resources from Woolworths Head Office to the Australian operation. Naturally the local Woolworths setup suffered as for various reasons the most suitable replacements were not easily available locally and the talent loss of Darren Todd, Woolworths head of technology and David Collins, head of Menswear to Country Road and David Jones boards respectively is only two examples of the strain that was placed on Woolworths.

For one, the acquisition of Australian department store David Jones shows little sign of delivering what was promised when the R22bn purchase was signed four years previously. On the contrary, the decision to impair David Jones by almost R7bn resulted in Woolworths posting a full-year loss of R3.5bn in 2018.

Woolworths' local fashion offering in 2018 was roundly rejected by its core 35-to 50-year-old customer base, and only its food division showed any real growth.

From my point of view, I believe that the major cause for the lack lustre performance was in simple terms that Woolworths changed its core strategy which in turn confused the loyal Woolworth's customer. Woolworths offering went from a singular brand and fragmented the presentation into a multitude of brands and rearranged the stores into a departmental format. The layouts of the store consisted of no less than nine options, each with their unique features and place in the store. For this reason, I was not surprised when I visited the Somerset Mall store and was confronted with a map on an easel in the aisle to assist me to find the David Jones, Country Road, Trenery, Mimco and the Woolworths stable consisting of Edition, RE, Studio W, JTOne many of which carried very similar product but with varying fits and styling.

As a result, Woolworths' local fashion offering was roundly rejected by its core 35-to 50-year-old customer base, and only its food division showed any real growth. The fact that the food division showed real growth indicates that the customers were available and are prepared to spend money as the division not only showed real growth in terms of more than 8% in sales and profit while the entire group only grew 1.6% to R75bn in 2018. While Foods formed 43% of the sales, because of the competitive margin policy only contributed 27% of the profit.

The Woolworths clothing division in fact showed a decrease of 1.5% decline in sales and a 4% decline in profit. It only contributed 20% of the group sales falling behind David Jones by 1% who delivered 21% contribution.

"Our womenswear modern range failed to resonate with our core customer," Woolworths CEO Ian Moir said in the results statement. While Investec analyst David Smith writes: *"Outside of Edcon, Woolworths has by far been the worst apparel performer of the large listed players in SA over the past 10 years … This … suggests the problem is more than just bad product."*

The South African clothes division contributed 20% of the group's sales, placing it behind David

Jones, which contributed 21%, with declined sales of 3.8% to R14.5bn and its gross profit down by 4.6% to R6.2bn.

THE WAY FORWARD
Recognising the failures in the performance woes in the financial year of 2018, the business had to take hard look at itself and in it's Annual Report highlights the strategic action that would be applied. In order to turn the situation around.

"We have six strategic focuses that we drive at a Group level which will deliver future-fit businesses that return to long-term profit growth and create sustainable value for all our stakeholders."

BUILD STRONGER, MORE PROFITABLE CUSTOMER RELATIONSHIPS
Our customer insights and data drive and inform all our business decisions as we become a more customer obsessed Group. To build on this, we continue to enhance our loyalty proposition and offer our customers a connected retail experience.

TOWARDS CONNECTED RETAIL
We focus on offering our customers inspiring, engaging and relevant digital and in-store journeys, helping our staff deliver a consistent, brand-aligned customer experience and connecting our customers seamlessly from our physical stores to our digital platforms and vice versa.

BE A LEADING FASHION RETAILER IN THE SOUTHERN HEMISPHERE
We differentiate ourselves on quality fashion that is relevant to our customers through clearly segmented, design-led, quality ranges and innovation.

BECOME A BIG FOOD BUSINESS WITH A DIFFERENCE
We are focused on providing our customers with consistent superior quality, flavour, safe, and innovative food at great value.

DRIVE SYNERGIES AND EFFICIENCIES ACROSS THE GROUP
We leverage our Group scale across the southern hemisphere, particularly within Australia. Through ongoing integration across business operations, we will drive efficiencies and maintain an absolute focus on cost control, adding significantly to Group profitability.

EMBED THE GOOD BUSINESS JOURNEY THROUGHOUT THE BUSINESS
Our Good Business Journey is our plan to make a difference for our people, in our communities, and for our environment. It encompasses the issues which matter most to our stakeholders and also enables a consistent approach to managing sustainability issues across our global supply chain. Our Good Business Journey facilitates us to achieve our vision to be one of the world's most responsible retailers.

After the failures with David Jones in Australia, Ian Moir informed the media that "Woolworths will be going back basics in its home market as it seeks corrective measures to lift it's poor trading performance. We've gone back to focus on the key items to build our ranges right and get the basics right. We are going back to being Woolworths rather than sub brands."

The Woolworths brand became too fashionable, appealing mainly for the 18 to 20-year-old segment which was the fundamental mistake as the core classic customer was catered for in the David Jones offering in stores.

Consequently, the David Jones label is being withdrawn from Woolworths stores and the classic product will return to be offered under the Woolworths label. Traditionally great basics is what Woolworths is renowned for consisting of the key and staple items in most wardrobes. This is the deep DNA of the business where foods got it spot on in 2018 while the clothing division lost the plot and plans need to be put firmly in place to regain the foundation that the company was established on right in the beginning under the watch of David Susman.

2019 is the last year that Simon Susman remains as Chairman and he is the final family connection to the founders of back in the day. He retires at the end of the AGM in 2019.

In his address at the 2018 AGM he said, "We've learnt a hell of lot of lessons and I am confident that within two years we will not be in the same situation."

Ironically, avoiding the same situation will be achieved by going almost full circle through the adoption of the rock steady principles and philosophies of the founding fathers.

Time will tell.

REFERRALS AND ACKNOWLEDGEMENTS

Max Sonnenberg: (1957) *The Way I saw it,* Howard Timmins (PTY) Ltd

Hugh McMillan: (2005) *An African Trading Empire,* I B Taurus, London

Tony Owen for his input on the local clothing industry

www.ingramcontent.com/pod-product-compliance
Lightning Source LLC
Chambersburg PA
CBHW030510220526
45464CB00006B/2742